The UFO was approaching . . .

As the boys' eyes adjusted to the brightness of the UFO, they could see colors of red and yellow flowing around the object like a field of energy.

Casey grabbed a flashlight. He aimed it at the UFO and turned it on.

"Are you crazy?" hissed Zack. "You'll point out exactly where we are."

"It doesn't matter," said Sam with a sense of doom in his voice. "They already know."

UFO
KIDS

by Allan Zullo
A NASH & ZULLO BOOK

Rainbow Bridge®
Troll Associates

*To my good friend, Bob Pratt, who will travel
to the ends of the earth in search of the truth
about UFOs.*

— Allan Zullo

LIBRARY OF CONGRESS CATALOGING-IN-PUBLICATION DATA

Zullo, Allan.
    UFO kids / Allan Zullo.
        p.   cm.
    "A Nash & Zullo book."
    ISBN 0-8167-3566-2 (pbk.)
    1. Unidentified flying objects—Sightings and encounters—Juvenile
literature.   [1. Unidentified flying objects.]   I. Title.
TL789.3.Z85   1995
001.9'42—dc20   94-27528

CONTENTS

ARE WE ALONE?

Are we humans the only intelligent beings in the universe? If we're not, then who are the others? Where are they? Have they visited Earth? Have they made contact with some of us?

Throughout the world, people from all walks of life have claimed they have experienced close encounters with UFOs and aliens from other planets. Kids have reported incredible incidents in which aliens terrorized them or even kidnapped them for a few horrifying hours. Other kids say they have made contact with friendly aliens who claim they want to help save our planet.

This book contains seven eerie stories based, in part, on cases taken directly from the files of noted experts who investigate UFO encounters. The names and places in these stories have been changed to protect everyone's privacy.

Are we alone? After reading this book, you be the judge.

THE BLACK RIVER ABDUCTIONS

For months, high school buddies Zack Myers, Casey Weller, and Sam Brighton had been planning a weekend canoeing and camping trip in Ontario, Canada. It was going to be the perfect adventure.

It ended up becoming a trip of a lifetime—one so mystifying and terrifying that they can't believe it really happened. In fact, they don't *want* to believe it really happened.

* * *

The 15-year-old boys had been dropped off on Friday night by Zack's father at a campsite along the Black River. The boys planned to pitch a tent for the night, then canoe down the river and occasionally stop to fish. They were going to camp again Saturday night and canoe farther before getting picked up Sunday afternoon about 20 miles (32 km) from where they first put in.

Although all three boys loved the outdoors, Zack and Casey enjoyed more physical activities such as rock climbing and backpacking than did Sam. In high school, Zack and Casey played football and starred on the sophomore wrestling team. Sam, on the other hand, was no athlete, even though he was built like one. He liked to write about sports and nature and hoped one day to be a TV newscaster. In fact, Sam brought along an audio cassette player and several blank tapes to record his impressions of the trip so he could write about it later. He also brought the tape recorder so they could use it to play their favorite music.

After they were dropped off, the boys eagerly pitched their tent and set up the gas camper stove. They boiled a pot of macaroni and heated up a jar of store-bought spaghetti sauce. They ate heartily, then headed off into the woods to collect firewood for the night.

"Before we build the fire, let's wait for it to get real dark and look at the stars," Sam suggested.

It was a great night for stargazing. The sky was clear and moonless, and the stars twinkled like diamond dust on black velvet. The boys walked to a sprawling meadow, lay down in the grass, and looked skyward.

"A dollar to the first one who spots a shooting star," said Casey. "But it's got to be a streaker that we all see."

"You know, if you let your imagination go, you can almost feel that you're looking down, not up," said Zack. "You can almost feel yourself floating."

"You know what's cool?" Sam added. "Mr. Langdon in science class was explaining about light years—that's the distance light travels in a year. It's awesome—

six trillion miles (9.6 trillion km). Mr. Langdon says that if a star is five light years away, that means it took the light from that star five years to get here. And there are stars that are *thousands* of light years away."

"That's so far away our brains can't compute it," said Casey.

Zack laughed and added, "The universe is so large, it's an eternity."

"I heard a neat description of eternity," said Sam, as he sucked on a long blade of grass. "Imagine a dove that flies once every million years to the moon and brushes its wing against the moon's surface. By the time the dove wears down the moon to the size of a marble, eternity has only just begun."

"Hey, my brain will go into overload if we keep talking like this," said Casey. "Let's talk about something really important, like Laura or Kristin or—"

Zack bolted up and pointed toward the north. "Hey, look at that!" A shooting star streaked across the sky, leaving a brilliant trail of blue-green light.

"Cool!" shouted Sam.

"Hey, I win a buck from you guys," said Zack.

"Why? I didn't see anything," Casey chuckled.

"The heck you didn't," retorted Zack. He stood up and offered Casey a light-hearted challenge: "Give me the dollar or I'll pin you."

"Let's wrestle," Casey said, springing to his feet.

While the two grappled with each other, Sam flicked on the flashlight and acted as the referee. Locking arms, the two wrestlers grunted and laughed, but neither could bring the other down.

Just then, something caught Sam's eye—a bright

orange ball of light low on the horizon. "Casey, Zack! Stop! Look at the sky!"

The three teens watched with awe as the round object, about the size of a jet plane, slowly angled up from behind a stand of pine trees about a half mile (.8 km) away from the boys. The orange glow pulsated like a mechanical heart, growing fainter and then brighter as it slowly climbed up.

"What's *that*?" asked Zack.

"It's not a shooting star, that's for sure," Casey said.

"It doesn't look like a plane," added Sam.

"Is it a helicopter?" asked Zack.

"There's no sound," Sam replied.

"Maybe it's a weather balloon," Casey suggested.

Just as the boys were ready to accept that explanation, they were stunned by a brilliant flash of light—like the strobe on a camera, only many times brighter. The light was so intense it hurt the boys' eyes and momentarily blinded them. They groaned and turned their heads away, waiting for their eyes to adjust again to the dark. When they looked back into the sky, the object had disappeared without a trace.

"Wow!" exclaimed Casey. "That was no balloon."

"What could it have been?" asked Zack.

"I don't have any idea," said Sam, "except . . . uh . . . you don't suppose . . ."

Casey gave a nervous laugh. "I know what you're going to say. That it might be a UFO."

"Well, it *could* be," said Sam. "Do you have a better explanation?"

"No, but . . ."

Suddenly, the boys' noses began itching, and they

smelled a horrible odor. "Man, that's disgusting," Casey declared with a gag.

"It's like rotten eggs," said Zack, holding his nose.

"It smells like sulfur," said Sam. "You know, that element we studied in chemistry class."

"It probably has something to do with that UFO or whatever it is we saw," said Casey.

"Could be," replied Sam. "The breeze is coming from that direction. And the smell is starting to go away."

"Maybe it was from the exhaust of that UFO," said Casey.

"If it *was* a UFO," Zack stressed. "Come on, let's get back to our camp."

As they headed toward their campsite, the boys kept silent, each lost in his own thoughts about what he had seen. Casey felt a mixture of excitement and fear because he was convinced he had just witnessed a UFO. Zack was trying to come up with some logical explanation other than a UFO. Sam was fighting a strange feeling that they were being watched. But he didn't say anything, because he didn't want his friends to think he was afraid.

"In the morning," said Casey, "why don't we go over to those trees where we first saw the UFO and snoop around."

"What do you expect to find?" asked Zack. "Little green men? And what would you do if you found them?"

"Look! To your right!" shouted Sam, in a high frightened voice. "Is that another UFO?"

"Are you talking about that firefly next to you?" asked Casey. He took a swipe at the lightning bug as he and Zack broke out in laughter at Sam's expense.

Sam responded by mumbling something about his "jerky" friends.

When they returned to their campsite, the three built a big fire and talked about what they had seen.

"I think I know what it was," said Zack. "I'll bet you it was a secret military spy plane. Yeah, that's what it was." He thought by saying it, he would believe his own words. But the truth was that he knew of no plane that could defy the laws of physics like that. Besides, his pals weren't buying his explanation.

"There's no reason to think we're the only ones in the universe," said Sam. "Mr. Langdon says there are more stars in the universe than grains of sand on Earth. Out of the billions and billions of stars out there, let's say only a million are the size of our sun. Out of those million, only a thousand have planets circling them. And out of those thousand, only a hundred have planets that are similar to Earth. Who's to say that those planets don't have air and water to support life?"

"And who's to say that life on other planets has to be like us?" said Zack. "Maybe they're weird beings like in *Star Trek* or *Star Wars*."

"Maybe they're friendly," said Casey.

"Maybe they're not," warned Zack. "If they can travel light years to get here, then they must be pretty smart. That means they probably have weapons and things that could wipe us out."

"Yeah, but if they're so advanced, maybe we're not worth bothering with," said Sam. "Maybe to them we're nothing more than bugs. Humans don't bother trying to communicate with ants, so maybe aliens don't want to bother with us."

"Hey, Zack, what would you do if you came face to face with a space alien?" asked Casey.

"I'd tell him to go visit your messy bedroom," Zack replied. "He'd get so freaked out, he'd leave the planet. Heck, he'd leave the galaxy."

"What about you, Sam?" asked Casey.

"I'd ask him to take me to his planet—as long as he brings me back. Then I'd hold a press conference and be part of the biggest story in the history of the world."

Then Casey asked, "How are you going to prove you were there?"

"I'll swipe one of their miniature transmitters or beaming devices, something like that."

The more they talked about space aliens, the more spooked Sam became, but he didn't want to let on to the others. So he yawned and said, "I'm really tired. I think I'm going to turn in."

"What for, Sam?" asked Casey. "Don't you want to talk some more about UFOs? Maybe we'll see another one."

"Or maybe we'll spot a UFI," said Zack.

Sam asked, "What's that?"

Recalling how earlier Sam had mistaken a firefly for a UFO, Zack wisecracked, "An Unidentified Flying Insect."

"Very funny," said Sam. "I'm turning in. I just can't keep my eyes open." It was a lie. Sam was starting to feel sick to his stomach because he had this weird feeling that the three of them were being watched. Talking about UFOs only made matters worse. He figured if he could just get into his tent and fall asleep, the eerie feeling would go away.

* * *

The next morning, the boys woke up at daybreak. There was a chill in the air. They fixed themselves some instant Cream of Wheat and toasted bread over the flame of their camper stove.

As Sam had feared, his feeling about being watched had not gone away. He began loading up the canoe and stayed busy so he wouldn't have to think about the UFO.

"Hey, Sam, don't load that stuff now," said Casey. "We need to go find that spot where the UFO took off."

"Come on, you're not serious are you?" asked Sam. "You're just going to waste time. We came here to canoe and fish, not look for a UFO landing site."

"Stay if you want," replied Casey. "But Zack and I are going over to that spot. We'll be back in an hour."

Casey and Zack walked off, leaving Sam alone. About 20 minutes later, the two teens reached the stand of pine trees where they had seen the UFO rise. They ambled around the trees, not really knowing what they were looking for.

"Hey, do you smell something?" Casey asked.

Zack took a deep breath. "Yeah, that sulfur smell from last night." As they walked farther into the woods, the odor grew stronger until they reached a small clearing. "Wow, look at this," said Zack, pointing to the ground. A rounded area about 20 feet (6 m) in diameter was blackened as though it had been charred. Zack bent down and touched the ground. It felt dry and warm as though it had recently been burned.

He picked up a handful of the ground and smelled it. "Yuck! It's like rotten eggs." Then he walked to an area that had not been burned and examined the ground. It was cool and moist and didn't smell.

"What do you think did this?" asked Casey.

"I don't know," Zack replied. "But whatever it was probably got the branches of those trees too." On the sides of the trees that ringed the burned area, the needles were brown, while the needles on the other side of the pines were green.

"Whatever it was, it had some powerful heat," said Casey.

Zack nodded and added, "I don't know whether to feel scared or excited."

"How about both."

* * *

Meanwhile, back at the campsite, Sam brought out his cassette player and plopped himself down on the riverbank. He inserted a blank tape and plugged in the microphone to record some of his thoughts. "When I look at the sky at night, I can't help but wonder if we're alone. I don't think we are. I mean, what makes us so special? Why should we be the only ones in the universe? There's room for all sorts of people . . . or aliens . . . or whatever they are. They don't have to look like us. Why should they?" The more he talked about space beings, the more Sam felt uneasy. He put the microphone down and stopped the tape player.

And then he heard: *"Don't be afraid."* It was an eerie, soft voice—not male or female. Even stranger, it seemed to be coming from Sam's own mind. Startled, he turned around, looking to his left and right and even gazing up. But he didn't see anyone.

"Nothing bad will happen," said the voice, still sounding like it came from inside his head.

"What's going on?" Sam asked out loud. "Casey? Zack? Is that you?" Silence. *Am I losing my mind?* he wondered. *Now I'm hearing voices. My imagination is running wild. I've got to put a stop to this UFO nonsense. I'm starting to act crazy.*

Trying to turn his attention to something else, Sam picked up a few flat stones. Then he began flinging them in the water, trying to see how many times he could make one skip across the surface.

"We mean you no harm," said the voice.

"Stop it! Stop it!" shouted Sam. He threw down the stones, clasped his hands over his ears, and ran to his cassette player. He popped in a Red Hot Chili Peppers tape and turned up the volume, hoping to drown out the voice in his head. Then Sam sat down on a rock and tried hard to think of nothing but the music. But he couldn't.

Why do I think I'm being watched? Why do I feel so weird? Why am I hearing a strange voice in my head? What's happening to me? Could that UFO have landed again? Are aliens out there right now? Could they be ready to snatch us at any moment? Could they —

Suddenly, from behind, two cold clammy hands gripped the tops of his shoulders. Sam let out a terrified yell and tried to leap off the rock. But the hands forced him back down. Paralyzed with fear, he slowly turned around. He kept his eyes nearly closed, afraid that what he was about to see would be the most frightening thing he could ever imagine. But what he saw turned his fear into rage. "You cheese heads!" he yelled.

The hands gripping his shoulders belonged to Zack and Casey, who had sneaked up behind him. The two teens were laughing so hard they fell to the ground. "We got you good!" shouted Casey, as tears streamed down his face.

"Very funny, you jerks. I was in deep thought and you surprised me, that's all."

When they stopped laughing, Zack and Casey told Sam about the smelly burned area they had found in the woods. But Sam didn't say a word about the voice in his head. He didn't want them to think he was going crazy . . . or, even scarier, that an alien had communicated with him.

* * *

After a full day of canoeing and fishing, the boys stopped for the night about 12 miles (19 km) downstream and set up camp again. They had caught their dinner—blue gill and smallmouth bass—and ate their entire catch. Much to Sam's relief, he didn't hear the voice anymore, and everyone seemed pretty much talked out about UFOs.

After the sun set, they decided to try some night fishing. They built a safe but blazing fire to mark their campsite so they could find their way back to it. Then they hopped into the canoe and drifted downstream. It was another clear night and the sky sparkled with stars.

About 10 P.M., Sam again felt this strange feeling that they were being watched. This time it was stronger than ever before. And then he heard the voice in his head: *We need you now.*

"Did one of you just say something?" he asked. Zack, in the middle of the canoe, and Casey, in front, shook their heads. "I didn't think so," he muttered to himself.

Sitting in the back of the canoe, Sam felt an urge to look behind him. When he did, he gasped. "Guys! Behind us! Look!" Hovering about 300 feet (90 m) over the river and a quarter mile (.4 km) away was the huge glowing UFO from the night before.

Slowly and silently, it neared the boys, whose horror and fascination increased as the object approached. As the boys' eyes adjusted to the brightness of the UFO, they could see colors of red and yellow flowing around the object like a field of energy.

Casey grabbed a flashlight. He aimed it at the UFO and turned it on.

"Are you crazy?" hissed Zack. "You'll point out exactly where we are."

"It doesn't matter," said Sam with a sense of doom in his voice. "They already know."

"Let's get out of here!" yelled Zack.

"It won't do any good," Sam replied.

Suddenly, a tube-shaped beam of blue light burst from the UFO, shot down to the water, and skimmed straight for the canoe. "Paddle! Paddle!" yelled Zack. Casey dug his paddle into the water and stroked furiously. But Sam didn't move a muscle. His eyes were locked on the beam as it moved closer to them.

Zack ripped the paddle from Sam's hand and began furiously stroking. "We're never going to outrun it!"

Now the blue beam was directly overhead. It bathed the three teens in a light that left them dumbfounded, unable to speak or hear anything. They felt a tingling sensation over their entire bodies and their muscles went limp. Slowly, the three were lifted out of their canoe by an unseen force and floated up into the tube of light toward the UFO.

Zack was crazed with fear. *What's happening? Who's doing this? This must be a dream. Please, someone tell me this is a dream!*

Meanwhile, Casey tried to struggle free, but he remained as slack as a rag doll. *I'm floating and nothing is holding me up. I could fall at any time. Why can't I move my muscles? I've got to get out of here!*

Sam gazed down and spotted their campfire below, appearing farther and farther away. He looked up and saw he was only a few yards from the underbelly of the UFO. *It's really happening. The aliens have come and they're taking us away! But why us?*

Suddenly, everything became a blur, and the boys all felt a dizzying sensation as if they had gone on one ride too many at the amusement park. The next moment, they were inside the craft in a room with dim red lights.

"Where are we?" cried Zack.

"We're inside the UFO," Sam blurted out.

"I'll fight them," snarled Casey, "if they so much as—"

He shut up when a door to the room slid open. The terror-stricken boys gasped when three human-like beings stepped into the room. Two of the beings stood about four feet (1.2 m) tall and one was about six inches (15 cm) shorter. They all had pencil-thin arms and legs that looked too long for their little rounded bodies. Their light-bulb-shaped heads were larger than a human's and sat on long slender necks. Their heads each had a small slit for a mouth, no nose but two holes for nostrils, and huge almond-shaped, dark green eyes. The eyes angled up toward two small holes on each side of the head that passed for ears. Their hands featured three slender, clawlike fingers. The aliens were dressed in tight-fitting gray bodysuits that closely matched the color of their skin.

"Don't be afraid," said the Short One. It was the same voice that Sam had heard earlier that day. "We won't hurt you." The alien's mouth didn't move, but he was able to communicate through each boy's mind.

"Please let us go," Sam pleaded. "We haven't done anything to you."

"You will be all right. Please come with us."

The Short One stared into Sam's eyes. When the teen stared back, he quickly felt like he had lost his will and was ready to follow the aliens. However, Casey and Zack chose not to cooperate.

"Stay away!" hissed Casey. "I'm warning you! Don't touch me. I'm bigger than you." The aliens moved to one side of the room and kept staring at him.

They're not blocking the door, he thought. *This is my chance.* Casey bolted for the open door and dashed down a passageway. He had no idea where to go or how to escape. He was winging it, hoping by some miracle that he'd find a way out.

While two of the aliens stayed with Zack and Sam, the other one simply walked after Casey who had come to a dead end. Frantically, the teen looked around for a new escape route. Just then, a nearby door slid open and another alien stepped out. Casey rushed by him and entered what looked like an examination room where two more aliens were working on a large device that looked like an x-ray machine. The aliens turned around when they saw him and calmly started to walk toward him.

"Don't be afraid," said one of the aliens. "We won't hurt you."

"Yeah, but I'll hurt you if you take another step toward me," Casey warned. Then he grabbed what looked like a glass rod off a counter and tried to break it so he could use its jagged edge as a weapon. He whacked the rod against the counter, but it wouldn't shatter.

"Please calm down," said the alien. "We mean you no harm." Eventually, two more aliens entered the room and slowly walked toward Casey, who kept backing up until his shoulders touched the wall. "You're trying to corner me, aren't you?" he said. "Well, take this!"

He charged into two of the aliens and knocked them down. As he dashed out into the passageway, he was amazed at what pushovers they were. They're not so tough, he thought. They're weaklings. Then he studied his situation. I'm in a hallway, there are more aliens walking toward me, and I don't know how to get out of here. They're going to get me, but I'm not going to give in—not without a fight.

Just then, a much taller being—over six feet (1.8 m) tall with a more oval-shaped head and larger eyes— walked into the hallway and confronted Casey. It stared directly into Casey's eyes until the teen felt his muscles go limp. The rod dropped out of his hand. *I'm losing my will to fight,* thought Casey. *What's it doing to me?*

"You could have caused serious problems if you had gone the wrong way," said the Tall One. "You could have killed yourself had you entered the room that controls our power source."

I feel so sluggish, Casey thought. *Why can't I move? I've got to fight. Concentrate—get your strength back.*

But his body refused to respond. Two of the smaller aliens then led a weakened Casey by the arms into the examination room.

Meanwhile, inspired by Casey's valiant effort, Zack warned the two aliens who were advancing on him, "I know karate and I'm a wrestler, so back off!" Zack began slicing the air with karate chops. "You're not going to get me!"

Two more aliens entered, and the four of them calmly tried to escort Zack into the passageway, but he fought them off. When they tugged at his arms, he pulled free and locked his arms around two handles on either side of the doorway.

"There's no reason to be difficult," said one of the aliens. "You must come with us."

"I'm not going anywhere with you!" he snarled. Although Zack was petrified, he sensed that the aliens were scared too. *What will they do if they're scared?* he wondered. *Will they shoot me with a ray gun? So what? Who cares? Let's find out.* "I'm not going through that door," he yelled at them. "Do you understand?"

The aliens were hesitant to do anything further to Zack, who seemed much stronger than they were. But then the Tall One came up from behind Zack, grabbed him by the head, and turned him until they were eyeball to eyeball.

Zack let out a scream and tried to wriggle free, but the Tall One was too strong for him. The alien just stared at Zack. In a matter of seconds the boy put down his hands and gave up.

"We are not going to hurt you," said the Tall One as he motioned the smaller aliens to take Zack into the examination room.

The Tall One then approached Sam, who had not moved a muscle out of sheer fear.

"Please relax," said the alien. "You are much too frightened when there is no reason."

"No reason?" said Sam. "You beam us up to a spacecraft against our will, and you tell us there's no reason to be scared?"

The alien didn't respond. Instead, he ordered Sam, "Follow me."

They walked into the examination room where Zack and Casey were sitting on tables surrounded by several aliens.

"What are you going to do to us?" asked Casey.

"A simple physical examination," the Tall One replied. Then, turning toward Casey and Zack, the Tall One said, "You shouldn't resist us like you did. You could get hurt." The alien started to stare again at Casey, who quickly closed his eyes. "Oh, no, not that trick again," said Casey.

Zack jumped off the table. "We can still fight them. Just don't look at him."

"Enough of this nonsense," said the Tall One. "If you cooperate, it will be much easier."

"For you maybe, but not for us," said Zack.

The Tall One turned to one of the aliens and talked to it in a sound and language that, to the teens, defied description. The Tall One then left the room.

The Short One, the first alien who had spoken to the boys, pointed to them and said, "We no longer need you. The examination will not take place."

"All right!" shouted Casey.

"Get me out of here," Zack added.

Sam breathed a big sigh of relief and murmured, "Thank you."

As they walked back toward the first room, Sam asked the Short One, "Why? Why did you take us?"

"Because you were there."

"You mean blind luck? We're going through this scary experience because we just happened to be in the area when you arrived?"

"Don't be upset," said the Short One. "It's all right. You won't remember any of this."

"Oh, this is something I don't think I'll ever, ever forget," said Sam.

"We have ways so you won't be burdened with remembering. We meant you no great inconvenience. The best way to eliminate any emotional trauma from this experience is to put a block on your memory of this incident. Please step toward me." He pulled out a device that looked somewhat like a telephone receiver.

But before the boys took a step, another alien ran into the room, said something that sounded urgent, and left.

The Short One turned to the teens and said, "You must go this instant. We will make you forget later." Suddenly, part of the middle of the floor opened, revealing a hole about five feet (1.5 m) in diameter.

The boys peered down and saw the tube-shaped beam of light that had floated them up into the craft. The beam was directly over their canoe about 300 feet (90 m) below.

"Please hurry," said the Short One. "Step forward and you will be returned."

"Whoa," said Sam. "I'm not going to jump into that hole. It's a long way down."

"You will not fall," said the alien. "You will float down. Go now before it's too late."

Sam took a deep breath, closed his eyes and stepped into the hole. To his surprise, he didn't fall. "Hey, look. I'm floating!"

"Hurry," said the alien.

The others gingerly put their feet out into the open space and felt an invisible force hold them. Then they found themselves floating down the hollow beam of light into their canoe. The beam held the canoe steady as each boy was placed in the same seating positions they were in before being taken aboard the craft.

The moment they were safely in their canoe, the beam vanished, a brilliant light flashed, and the orange UFO disappeared. Then they heard the screeching of two fighter jets zoom overhead. For several minutes, the boys remained in a state of shock, unable to move as the canoe floated downstream until it bumped into a thick branch of a tree growing from the bank.

Once they recovered from their shock and cleared the cobwebs from their minds, the stressed-out teens paddled back to their campsite. "The aliens must have dumped us off quick because they knew the jets were after them," said Zack. "I don't think those jets will ever catch them."

"What do you say we pack up and get out of here before those space beings find us again?" said Casey.

"It's not going to do us any good," Sam replied. "They'll find us no matter where we are."

"Why would they try?" asked Casey. "They don't need us anymore."

"They'll be back to wipe out our memory of tonight," Sam answered. "Remember what the Short One said, 'We will make you forget later.' They'll be back. We've got to tape record this before they make us forget it ever happened."

For the next hour the boys took turns recalling, in chilling detail, everything that had happened to them since they first spotted the UFO.

* * *

The boys woke up the next morning with splitting headaches. "Man, did I have a weird dream," said Casey. "I don't remember much about it, except I was fighting a bunch of people. Then I couldn't move. I felt helpless like I was under some spell."

"That's funny," Sam said. "I had a bad dream too. I was trapped in a room and I couldn't move."

"This is creepy," said Zack. "I had a nightmare where I was battling a pair of huge eyes."

"Must be the fish we ate last night," said Casey. "Hey, Sam, put on some music while I fire up the stove."

"What do you want? Red Hot Chili Peppers, Crash Test Dummies or, hey, what's this?" Sam looked at the label on one of the tapes. Scrawled on the cassette was the word UFO.

"Who's UFO? I've heard of U2 but not UFO."

"I don't know," replied Casey. "It's not my tape."

"Mine either," Zack added. "Why don't you play it?"

28

Sam popped the cassette into the tape recorder, expecting to hear music. But he and his pals were stunned by what they heard.

"This is Sam, along with Zack and Casey," came a trembling voice. "I know this is going to be hard to believe, but it's the honest truth. We were just beamed aboard a UFO by aliens from space. We're talking into this tape recorder because we're afraid they're going to wipe away our memories . . ."

The boys stared at each other in open-mouth amazement over what they were hearing. The tape recorder revealed each boy's version of their unbelievable experience aboard the UFO. When the tape ended, they slumped to the ground, totally astounded.

"Do you remember any of this?" asked Sam.

The other two shook their heads.

"This can't be a joke," he said. "All of our voices are on it."

"That explains our dreams and headaches," said Zack.

"Then it all really happened!" said Casey.

"They must have come back some time during the night and wiped it out of our memories," said Zack.

"Yeah, but we fooled them," said Sam. "We wouldn't let them make us forget."

THE ALIEN HEALER

Ten-year-old Mandy Williams couldn't run and jump and play hard like normal kids. She suffered from a serious disability—a heart valve that had failed to develop properly. As a result, she got tired easily. Any kind of physical activity often made her dizzy and out of breath.

For years, doctors kept a close watch on Mandy's heart until the decision was made to operate on her. The surgery would be risky, the doctors said, but it was the only way they could save her life.

"I don't know what it feels like to be normal," said the blond fourth grader. "But if you can make me better, let's go for it."

The operation was scheduled to take place in two months because the doctors wanted Mandy to recover fully from a bad cold that, in her condition, could be life-threatening. They also hoped she would gain weight, which would help her recover from the surgery.

But Mandy never had the operation—at least, not the kind anyone expected.

* * *

One wintry night, about 11:30 P.M., Mandy was tossing and turning in bed in her New Hampshire house. Since she couldn't get to sleep, she turned on the TV in her room. She wasn't really watching it, just listening to MTV with her eyes shut.

Suddenly she heard a high-pitched humming sound. She opened her eyes and looked around the room. She thought it might be coming from the TV set, so she turned it off. But the annoying sound didn't stop. Mandy began getting an uneasy feeling. A creepy feeling.

She looked out her first-floor bedroom window and didn't see anything unusual. There were no tracks in the freshly fallen snow. Still, she felt there was someone outside the window—and it was giving her the chills. She made sure the window was locked and pulled down the shade.

The humming sound wouldn't go away, so Mandy threw the pillow over her head. When that didn't help, she decided to wake up her parents. As she got out of bed, she saw a streak of blue light flash through the window shade.

I don't want to look at the window anymore, she told herself. *I don't want to stay here.* She walked out of her room with a feeling that twisted her stomach in knots. *Something bad is about to happen to me.*

Mandy wanted to run to her parents' bedroom, but she couldn't because of her condition. She already felt light-headed from worry, which was putting a strain on her heart. When she finally entered her parents' doorway, she cleared her throat and announced, "Mommy, Daddy, I'm scared."

"What's the matter, sweetheart?" asked her mother.

"I have a creepy feeling," Mandy replied. "There's a humming sound coming from my room."

Her father got out of bed and checked her room. "Everything seems fine," he said when he returned.

"You didn't hear that humming sound?" she asked. "You didn't see a blue flash?"

"No."

"Maybe you were dreaming," said her mother.

"No, I was awake because I never got to sleep. I'm scared and I don't know why." Mandy clutched her chest. "My heart is pounding so fast."

"Did you take your medicine?" her mother asked.

Mandy nodded.

"Would you like to sleep with us tonight?"

"I know it's silly, but I think I'd like that. First, I need to go to the bathroom."

As she walked down the hall, she saw another flash of blue light. It startled her so much that she let out a yelp.

"What's the matter, Mandy?" said her father, leaping out of bed.

"Daddy, Mommy, did you see it? It was like lightning, only it wasn't. It flashed inside the house, not outside. Something isn't right. Something bad is going to happen! I just know it!"

After her father again searched the house and found nothing, her mother told her, "Sweetheart, come to bed with us. Maybe that new heart medication you're on is playing bad tricks in your head."

Mandy climbed into bed with her parents, snuggling in between them. She pulled the covers tight against her chest and felt a little safer. Within a matter of minutes, her worry was replaced by sleep.

In the wee hours of the morning, Mandy once again heard the humming sound as she stirred from a deep sleep. Soon, a tingling sensation numbed her arms and spread to her chest, legs, and feet. Then Mandy felt like she was floating out of the bed. She wanted to open her eyes, but couldn't. She wanted to speak, but couldn't. In fact, she was virtually paralyzed. Even her mind seemed to shut down, neither questioning nor wondering what was happening to her.

While the floating sensation continued, she felt cold and started to shiver. Then she caught a whiff of smoke from burning wood. Moments later, she stopped shivering and warmed up again. With the humming sound ringing in her ears, Mandy had the feeling that she was lying on a metal table. Next, she felt something sharp, like a knife, scraping against her right arm and then a fingernail being clipped on her right hand.

No matter how hard she tried, Mandy still couldn't open her eyes or move her muscles. And she still didn't have the will to wonder what was going on.

She then felt two short, painful jabs in her left forearm that stung for several seconds. This was followed by a sensation of being poked in the ribs and heart with the eraser end of a very fat pencil. Three small areas right over her heart began to heat up almost to the point of burning before they cooled down.

Eventually, Mandy felt herself floating, shivering, and finally warm again under the sheets of her bed. The tingling sensation left and she fell fast asleep.

The next morning, when Mandy woke up, she felt as though she had hardly slept at all. She vaguely remembered dreaming about floating. For a reason she couldn't understand, she still had an uneasy feeling.

While she was toweling off after taking a shower, Mandy looked in the mirror and noticed three reddish circles, each about the size of a dime, right over her heart. The circles formed a triangle, two on the bottom, one on top. They didn't itch or hurt, although they did feel slightly warmer than the rest of her skin. *Where did they come from?* Mandy wondered. *I never noticed them before. I hope they're not a sign that something else is wrong with my heart.*

She called her mother into the bathroom to look at the circles. "I've never seen anything like this," said her mom. "Maybe it's a rash or a reaction to the new medication you're taking. It looks like something was pressing on your chest and left an impression."

"Last night I had the strangest dream, except there were no pictures," said Mandy. "It was all dark. I heard a humming sound, and I felt someone poking me around my heart right where those circles are."

"Let's keep an eye on it. If it doesn't go away or gets worse by later in the day, we'll call Dr. Pennington."

As she looked over her body for other circles, Mandy spotted two small marks on her left forearm near the elbow. "Mom, look at this," she said, pointing to the scabs. "In my dream I felt jabbing in my arm. And, oh yeah, I also felt scraping against my arm. Look."

Sure enough, a four-inch (10-cm) patch of skin beyond her right wrist was raw and flaky. "I just remembered one other thing. I had a fingernail clipped in my dream." She held up her right hand and spread her fingers. The nail on her index finger had been clipped. "Mom," said Mandy with a worried look spreading across her face, "I didn't have any of these things when I went to bed last night."

"I don't understand," her mother replied. "You spent the night in our bedroom with us."

"Not according to my dream."

* * *

The next night, as Mandy got ready for bed, she again had the jitters and didn't know why. She just didn't feel safe, but knew she couldn't ask to sleep with her parents again. *I'm a big girl now, ten years old,* she told herself. *I shouldn't be afraid of going to bed alone. I'll keep my bedroom door open, though.*

Rather than watch television, Mandy read a book in bed, hoping that would ease her troubled mind and make her fall asleep. Every once in a while, she would stop reading and listen carefully for that awful humming sound. But all was quiet. Shortly after 11 P.M., Mandy was so tired that she turned off the light and fell asleep.

About 3 A.M., Mandy woke up with a start. Her TV set was on, displaying the electronic snow from a station that had signed off for the night. Groggily, she reached for the remote control by her bed and turned it off. But seconds later, the TV turned back on. She aimed her remote at the set again to shut it off. But it didn't do any good. The TV sprang to life.

I guess I'll have to unplug it, she thought. Just as she threw back her covers, she began to hear the same high-pitched humming from the night before. "Oh, no, not that sound again!" she said out loud. A wave of terror washed over Mandy—a strong feeling that somebody was watching her. Trembling from fear, Mandy pulled the covers over her head because she was too scared to look.

Somebody is in my room! I can feel it. Somebody is standing right by my bed. Mandy, you're scaring yourself. Get a grip, girl. Just turn over and look. No one is there. Oh, I don't know if I can. What if somebody is in my room? What will I do?

With her heart beating faster and faster, Mandy slowly peeked from under the covers. She gasped in horror at what she saw. At the foot of her bed were three small beings. About as tall as a yardstick, the beings had brownish, chalky skin, big heads, and large slanted eyes. They wore dark, skin-tight uniforms and boots. While two of them floated a few inches off the floor, the leader glided over to the petrified girl—who was too numb to move or speak—and gently placed his hand on top of her head.

Immediately, her racing heart slowed down and the incredible fear that was surging through her body eased, but only slightly.

"Who—who are you?" she finally managed to stammer.

"We need you to come with us," replied the leader. He didn't talk with his mouth, but Mandy could hear him through her mind. "We will be gone for only a short while."

"No. I'll scream," she said defiantly. She filled her lungs to yell for help when the leader again touched Mandy's head. The girl exhaled without screaming.

"What are you going to do to me?"

"We're going to help you."

"I don't want your help," she snapped.

The other two beings moved over to the opposite side of the bed and stared at her while the leader placed both hands on Mandy's head. Within a few seconds, her mind went blank and her arms and legs began to tingle just as they had the previous night. Her limbs became paralyzed.

"You're going to float now, but don't be scared," said the leader. "Everything will be all right."

Her eyes darting wildly, Mandy watched helplessly as she drifted up and out of her bed and, in a standing position, floated with her three intruders through the window, which had mysteriously been opened. Although floating like this seemed an impossible feat, her mind accepted it.

She felt cold from the wintry night air and smelled smoke lingering from the chimneys of nearby homes—the same sensations she had experienced in her dream the previous night. When Mandy looked down, she saw her house getting smaller and smaller. Then she gazed up and saw a large hovering space-craft encircled with blue lights.

Before she knew it, Mandy was lying on a metal table inside a small circular room bathed in bright yellow light. The chamber was empty of any other furniture, windows, or things on the wall. Mandy sat up and looked at the three beings who stood, or rather floated, by her side.

"Am I in a spaceship?" she asked.

"Yes," replied the leader.

"This isn't a dream, is it?

"No."

"I was here last night, wasn't I?"

"Yes."

"I remember floating, getting cold, smelling smoke, and then lying on a table and getting poked. Why didn't I get to see anything then?"

"For your safety and comfort. We didn't want you to be frightened."

"Oh, like I'm not right now," she said sarcastically.

"We can ease your mind." He started to walk toward her, but she held up her hand and said, "Don't touch me. The last time you did, I turned into a zombie."

The leader backed off and said, "We will not harm you."

Nothing more was said for several minutes, and Mandy got the impression that they were waiting for someone else to show up. She used the time to study the small beings.

Their hairless heads, shaped roughly like rounded diamonds, seemed much too large for their bodies. They had no nose or ears. Their huge dark eyes were the single most striking feature about them. The eyes started about halfway down the face and angled up toward where the ears would be if they had them. Mandy noticed that their eyes had no pupils—the black hole in the center of the human eye—or eyebrows. The eyes didn't move from side to side or blink.

The aliens had a slit for a mouth and no lips. The

mouth didn't move and looked to Mandy like nothing more than a small straight line made by a felt-tipped pen. For a nose, the alien face had a slightly raised bump but no nostrils or openings.

The three aliens in the room looked so much like triplets that she couldn't tell one from another. One thing she didn't like about them was that they showed no changes in their expressions. There was no way of telling if they were happy or sad, angry or pleased. Their eyes didn't give any hint of emotions.

The aliens' arms were long, tubelike, and very thin as though they had no real muscles. The arms were the same size in diameter at the shoulder as they were at the elbows and at the wrists. Their hands and fingers resembled a human's, although they were unusually stubby. Mandy counted three fingers on each of their hands.

Their brownish-gray skin was smooth and hairless and had no freckles, wrinkles, spots, or bumps. After studying them, Mandy said to the leader, "This might sound weird, but can I touch you?"

He moved closer to her, and she timidly tapped the back of his hand with her finger as if she were touching the burner of a stove to see if it was heating up. She decided to try again, this time with her hand, for a few seconds longer. His skin felt soft, rubbery, and warm.

"Interesting," she said. "It feels like one of my old dolls."

Just then a much taller alien, with grayer skin and even larger eyes, entered the room. The other aliens moved away as he approached Mandy. She took an instant dislike to him and felt afraid of him. He stared at her intently, and she meekly leaned back until she was lying down on the table. It was as if she had been ordered to do so even though the alien said nothing to her. When she tried to sit up, she felt restrained by invisible straps. She wanted to move her arms and legs, but she was paralyzed.

"What did you do to me?" she cried out. "Let me up!"

"Don't be frightened," he said in her mind. "We're going to make you well again."

"What do you mean? What are you going to do?"

The table was then moved into another chamber that looked somewhat like the operating room of a hospital. As she turned her head to the left, she saw several large machines similar to monitors and x-ray equipment.

Mandy looked to the right and, to her surprise, saw a teenage boy lying down on a table on the other side of the room. His head was turned toward her. He had the build of a football player and the eyes of a frightened puppy.

"Don't let them stick anything up your nose!" he yelled at Mandy in a hoarse, trembling voice. He spoke rapidly as if he knew the aliens would quickly shut him up. "It's a locating device so they can find you whenever they want. But it makes you forget that you have it. I've been brought here before so —" He never finished the sentence. One of the short aliens had rushed over to him, placed both hands on the boy's head, and silenced him.

Fear jangled every nerve in Mandy's body, and she let out a loud shriek. The tall alien bent over and placed his hand firmly on Mandy's forehead. When he released his hand, she couldn't utter a sound or move

40

her head. "We're not trying to hurt him, you, or the others we've examined," the alien said to Mandy. "But sometimes there is discomfort. It can't be helped."

He reached for a slender tweezer-like instrument that, at the tip, held a tiny metal ball smaller than a BB. The alien then gently placed the tweezers into and high up Mandy's nose.

No, no! I don't want you sticking that up my nose! Mandy cried out in her mind. Again she tried to struggle and scream, but was helplessly paralyzed. *It's starting to hurt. Ouch! It feels like it's going up into my head. It hurts! Take it out! Take it out!*

Much to her relief, he removed the tweezers. The pain began to go away, but the inside of her nose next to her right eye remained extremely sore. Uh, oh, she thought. I don't see that little BB. Where is it? Don't tell me you left that BB inside my nose. You did, didn't you?

"What was done was necessary to help us," said the alien. "And what is about to be done is necessary to help you."

A large machine with a video screen was placed over Mandy's body. A light, like one in a dentist's office, beamed down on her. The light shined on her head and then moved down to her chest, stomach, legs, and feet. As it moved over her body, Mandy could see on the video screen her internal organs— her brain, heart, stomach, and intestines. The beam went back over her heart and stayed there as the alien studied the screen for several minutes.

What are you going to do now? Not my heart! Please don't do anything to my heart. I'm going to have an operation in a couple of months. You'll hurt me. I hate this. I don't want to be here. Can I go home now? Please?

The alien took a rod-shaped device with a glowing red light on the tip and placed it on her chest above her heart. The device began to vibrate and make a buzzing sound. That's not bad, she thought. It kind of tickles.

Next, the alien used a gadget that reminded Mandy of a flashlight and aimed it at her heart. A bright, pencil-thin green light hit her chest, and she quickly felt the area around her heart warm up. *You're doing something to my heart. Please don't. Leave me alone. Stop it! Stop it! Why can't I move? Why are you doing this to me?*

"To make you well again."

You can read my mind?

"Yes," said the alien. "But you must relax. You are becoming stressed and that's not good for your heart."

How can I relax when you're playing around with my heart? Please let me go.

"We can't until we are finished."

What are you doing now? He put a helmet over her head that completely covered her face, plunging her into darkness and cutting off her air supply. *No! No! I can't see! I can't breathe! Don't kill me, please don't kill me!* But then cool, fresh, sweet air flowed into her nose. Next, soft pretty lights came on inside the helmet and switched from one beautiful color to another. Within a few seconds, Mandy was totally relaxed and completely free of any kind of feeling. She couldn't tell where her fingers and toes ended. It was as if she had melted away, as if she were part of the air herself.

Mandy lost all track of time. Maybe a second later or maybe hours later—she had no idea—the helmet was removed.

Is it over? Are you done? Am I okay?

The alien put his hands on both sides of her face and with his three fingers gently massaged her temples. Suddenly, Mandy felt in control of her arms, legs, and the rest of her body. She immediately pressed her hands on her chest over her heart to feel for any pain. There was none.

"You may sit up now," the alien said. "I'm finished."

"What did you do to me?" she asked, relieved that she could once again talk.

"You will find out. Get off the table and walk around the room for me."

Mandy carefully slid off the table, afraid that she would feel dizzy when she stood up. But she felt fine. She walked around the table and noticed a remarkable change in her body. She felt perky and more energized than she had ever felt before. Her entire body felt warmer. Her hands, which always had been slightly cold and blue from her heart condition, were warm and pink. She walked around the table a little faster while the alien watched.

"How do you feel?" he asked.

"Great," she replied with wonder. "I feel bouncy and warm all over, and I'm not short of breath or dizzy or anything like that. What did you do to me?"

"Just what had to be done."

"Well, whatever you did, thanks. Can I go home now?"

"Yes."

In her excitement and relief that her ordeal was nearly over, she had forgotten about the boy on the examining table on the other side of the room. She looked over at him. While one alien was lightly scraping skin samples off his left arm, another was drawing blood from his right arm. *That's what they did to me last night.* And then a horrible thought dawned on her. *If he's been brought back here before, does that mean I will too?*

"Hey, wait," she said to the alien. "I've got a question for you."

But she never got to ask it. The same three aliens who had escorted her to the spacecraft hustled her into another room. They had her sit in an egg-shaped chair where she promptly fell asleep. When Mandy woke up, she was in her own bed, but with her feet on the pillow and her head at the foot of the bed.

Groggily, she started for the bathroom when vivid images from a few hours earlier flooded her mind. It dawned on her that either she had experienced the most bizarre dream of her life or else something unbelievable had happened to her. *I don't know if I want it to be a dream or not,* she told herself. *If it is a dream, there's nothing to worry about. If it's real, I should feel better. But that would mean I was operated on by real aliens! Ooh, that gives me the shivers. Well, there's only one way to find out.*

Mandy's heart was once again pounding wildly. As she entered the bathroom, she realized that she hadn't experienced any of the usual dizziness she usually felt when she first woke up. *Is it possible I had heart surgery in a spaceship?* She stood in front of the bathroom mirror, opened her nightgown, and stared at her chest. Mandy gasped. The three circles were gone. Instead, a small, red, inch (2.5 cm) wide, circular mark like a bicycle wheel with spokes appeared directly over her heart.

Well, if my heart is better, then I should be able to do things I've never done before. Cautiously, she jumped two inches (5 cm) off the floor. Then she did it again and again, higher and higher. *I'm not dizzy! I'm not weak! I can jump!* She started jogging in place. *My heart is working fine. It's fixed!* She threw up her hands like a professional athlete, danced around the bathroom, and yelled, "Yes! Yes!"

Suddenly Mandy stopped. Reality set in. She gripped the sides of the sink to hold herself steady from the shock. *Uh-oh. I've just been operated on by an alien from space! I sure hope he's a good doctor. And what if they come back for me? Like there's really something I can do about it! But, hey, my heart feels strong. I'm well! But now what do I do? What do I say to Mom and Dad? Nothing, Mandy. Don't say anything about the operation. They'll be scared if they believe me, and they'll think I'm crazy if they don't. I'll just pretend it didn't happen. But I've got to say something. This is the greatest news in the world!*

At the breakfast table, Mandy gave both her parents a big hug and a kiss followed by a happy "Good morning!"

"My, aren't you Little Miss Sunshine today," said her smiling mother.

"I feel real good today," Mandy announced. "Except for this stuffy nose, I feel better than ever. Look!" She hopped a couple of times.

"Mandy! Stop that!" her father cried out. "Your heart!"

"My heart feels great. I think it's getting better."

* * *

A week before her scheduled heart operation,

Mandy sat in the office of Dr. Marsha Pennington and announced, "I don't need the surgery."

"But, honey, you do. You have a damaged heart."

"I feel fine, honest."

Dr. Pennington looked at Mandy's hands. "My, your hands are warm and you have excellent color under your fingernails. Let me listen to your heart." The doctor placed her stethoscope on Mandy's chest, expecting to hear the distinctive sound made by the defective heart valve. Instead, she heard the sound of a healthy valve. "Hmm, there must be something wrong with my stethoscope." The doctor used another one. "Well, that's odd."

Dr. Pennington then tested Mandy's blood pressure, which had always hovered near the danger zone. It was perfect. "I don't understand. Mandy, can you hop a couple of times?"

"I can do better than that." Mandy began running in place with all the vigor of a track star.

Dr. Pennington shook her head in amazement and declared, "This is unbelievable! We've got to run more tests!"

A few hours later, after Mandy had undergone an EKG, an ultrasound, and a treadmill test, the results were in.

"Mandy, I've gone over your tests—and I'm stunned," said Dr. Pennington. "In fact, I called in two other heart specialists to study the results, and they confirmed my conclusion. Your heart is fine and the valve is working great—and I can't explain why. You were a very sick girl whose heart was about to fail. And now it's healthy. I don't know what to say except that this is a miracle."

Mandy grinned and said, "I guess you could say it's out of this world!"

THE HARDEN RANCH INTRUDERS

When the Harden family—Dennis, Joan, and their two teenage children Becky and Brett—agreed they'd had enough of the big city, they decided to change their lifestyle in a dramatic way. They sold their house in Chicago, where Dennis worked in the meat-packing industry, and bought a small cattle ranch on the great plains of Wyoming in the foothills of the Rockies.

The Hardens expected long, hard, but rewarding hours of work, brutal winters and spectacular summers, and a safe and simple life. What they didn't expect was living on a ranch targeted for animal research—by visitors from another world!

* * *

Becky, 14, and Brett, 13, were eager to make the move out west because they loved riding horses and enjoyed the great outdoors. They pitched in to help their parents fix up the old ranch house, barn, and stable. They cleaned out the pond behind the stable, helped haul away rusty old farm machinery, and repaired the wire fence around the ranch. It was back-breaking sweaty work. But at the end of the summer, Becky, Brett, and their parents were thrilled with all they had accomplished.

What Becky and Brett loved most of all about their new life was riding their horses on the open plains and gazing at the beautiful Big Horn Mountains in the near distance. Every day, they rode out to check their livestock: beef cattle known as Herefords that grazed on the short, tough grass. The teens would gallop through the meadows and into the foothills. The air seemed so pure; the sky so wondrous. Little did they know that the sky held a startling secret.

Occasionally, when the entire family went out for an evening ride on their horses, they would see something bright in the sky that appeared bigger than a star and moved faster than an airplane. They didn't think much about it because the objects seemed so far away, so harmless. The Hardens figured they were looking at orbiting satellites or exhaust from high-flying jet fighters. They never gave serious thought to UFOs—that is, until Becky became the first in her family to encounter one.

It happened during an after-dinner ride on Dusty, her palomino. Becky had gone out looking for their collie Blaze, who hadn't been seen all day. That was strange because the dog almost always stayed close to the house.

About half a mile (.8 km) away, Becky, who had been calling Blaze's name, heard barking and growling coming from the other side of a ridge. "Blaze, is that you?" she shouted. "Here, boy! Come here, Blaze."

As she approached the ridge, she expected to see her dog running toward her. Instead, Becky gawked at a sight so startling she nearly fell off her horse. She yanked hard at the reins, and Dusty reared up and whinnied in fright.

Rising from the other side of the ridge was a large, glowing red craft shaped like the top of a lighthouse. Becky watched with amazement as it rose 1,000 feet (300 m) into the air and began making a whirring sound that hurt her ears. Then it swooped down to the right and headed straight toward her.

As she backed up her horse, Becky thought, *This isn't a plane or a helicopter. This isn't anything I've ever seen. It doesn't even look like it's from this world.* The red glow from the 50-foot- (15-meter-) wide craft grew in intensity and lit up the ground even though it was twilight outside. *I don't like the looks of this at all.*

"Blaze! Blaze! Where are you?" she shouted. "Come here, boy! Please, hurry!" She desperately wanted to stay and wait for Blaze, but the mysterious object was closing in on her. Dusty reared up again, and that was Becky's cue to get out of there fast.

"Come on Dusty," she said. "Let's high-tail it. Now!" Dusty didn't need any kick in the ribs to get going. He galloped toward the ranch house with the speed of a Kentucky Derby winner. As Becky and her horse streaked across the range, she kept glancing over her shoulder. There was no doubt about it. The UFO was following her from about 100 feet (30 m) in the air and half a football field (46 m) away.

"Hurry, Dusty! Hurry!" The ranch house was in sight now, and Becky took one last look behind her. The UFO had not gained on her, even though it was obvious that it had the power to overtake her at any moment. As soon as Becky neared the house, she jumped off, slapped Dusty on the rump, and yelled, "Get into the stable!" Then she burst into the house and screamed, "Mom! Dad! Brett! Come quick! There's a UFO outside!"

The rest of her family raced to the window and saw the object, about the size of three city buses side by side, hovering over the pond and casting a weird red glow on the water.

"I don't believe what I'm seeing," said Dennis.

"What is it?" Joan asked.

"I don't have the foggiest idea," he replied.

"It's a UFO!" declared Brett. "That's what it is!"

The circular object began flashing bluish-green lights. It continued to make an annoying high-pitched, sing-song noise that disturbed the horses in the stable and made the Hardens cover their ears.

"Oh, my gosh!" said Brett. "Look at the window!" The large living room window in front of them began to crack—one long jagged line that inched across the glass from the upper right to the lower left. "It must be from that awful sound," Brett said.

The Hardens stood motionless for several minutes, uncertain what to do. Then the craft began to move. It hovered over each of the ranch's outbuildings—the stable, the barn, the tool shed.

"Dennis, what are we going to do?" Joan asked.

"Stay inside and maybe it'll go away," he said.

"Let's call the sheriff's office," she suggested.

"And say what? 'There's a UFO over our ranch, and we want you to chase it away?' They'll think we're crazy."

"Well, I'm calling anyway," she said. No sooner had Joan reached for the phone than the whole house shook with a deafening sonic boom.

"It's gone!" shouted Brett. "One second it's here and the next it's disappeared just like that," he declared, snapping his fingers.

"Oh no!" Becky cried out.

"What's the matter, Becky?" asked Brett.

"Blaze! I forgot all about Blaze. We have to go back and get him."

"It's okay," he replied. "I see him coming now. He's walking kind of funny."

The entire family raced out of the house to greet their missing dog. He was trotting but not quite in a straight line, almost like he was dazed. When he saw the Hardens, he gave a happy yelp—and then collapsed on the ground.

"Blaze! What's wrong?" said Becky, who was the first to reach him. He looked up with glassy eyes, whimpered, and wagged his tail weakly. "Poor Blaze. What happened to you?" Carefully, Becky examined him for broken bones or evidence of a snakebite. Instead, she found several strange markings on him.

"Hey, look at this," she said, pointing to Blaze's collar. It was charred in the back. She parted the hair on Blaze's neck and found a fresh X-shaped scar.

"His ear has been clipped," added Brett. "It looks like someone took a scissors and cut a piece out of his ear, but there's no blood."

"And his eyes are extremely bloodshot," added Becky. "Who could have done this?"

They would soon learn the astounding answer.

* * *

The next morning, Blaze seemed as frisky and happy as ever. His eyes sparkled and his nose was cold and wet. He even had a little bounce in his walk.

"Only *he* knows what happened to him yesterday—and he isn't talking," said Brett as he and the rest of the family saddled up their horses.

"I'll tell you one thing," added Becky. "Whatever it was, I'm guessing that UFO was involved."

The Hardens decided to examine the spot where Becky first saw the UFO. Blaze tagged along, but when they were a few hundred yards from the ridge, he refused to go any farther. He sat down, whining and barking. Despite their urging, he wouldn't go near the ridge.

"He's definitely spooked by something," said Becky. "I admit, I'm a little spooked too. What if we find some space people . . . you know, from another planet?"

"We'll invite them home for ice cream and cake," joked Brett.

When they reached the crest of the ridge and looked down on the other side, Becky pointed to a spot and shouted, "There! Look at the grass!"

In a circular area roughly the size of a Little League baseball diamond, the range grass was completely matted down. It looked like some powerful force had blown the grass over so violently that it couldn't stand up.

"What do you think did this, Dad?" asked Brett.

Dennis scratched his head in bewilderment and replied, "Something beyond my understanding."

"It had to be caused by the UFO I saw," Becky said excitedly.

"Do you think it will come back?" asked Brett.

"Let's hope not," Joan answered.

* * *

When the Hardens returned to their ranch, Brett looked at the goat pen and exclaimed, "The goats are gone!"

"That's strange," said Dennis as he examined the gate. "The gate is still locked. How could they have gotten out?"

"I'll go look for them," said Brett. "I'll take Blaze with me."

Brett hopped on his black and white spotted horse, Checkers, and followed Blaze, who had quickly picked up the scent of the four missing goats. About a half hour later, he found them. They were huddled together and bleating fearfully.

Brett went up to the goats to see why they were acting so strange. "What's this?" he asked out loud. Each of the animals had a brown spot about two inches in diameter at the base of their neck. When Brett looked closer, he saw the same X-shaped scar that was on Blaze's neck. He looked at their eyes and noticed they were bloodshot. An ear of each goat had been cut, yet there was no sign of any blood. Brett examined the goats for any other markings and discovered that their tails had been cut with a sharp instrument. But, like their ears, the ends of their tails didn't have a single drop of blood.

Just then, Blaze began barking and whining, and the goats acted even more agitated than before.

Brett put his foot in the stirrup and was ready to mount his horse when out of nowhere the same UFO the family had seen the night before appeared directly in front of him.

Checkers reared up, throwing Brett to the ground, and took off in a frantic gallop. "Checkers!" shouted Brett, rubbing his backside as he got to his feet. "Wait! Get back here!"

The whirring, whining sound from the UFO screamed with such intensity that he felt dizzy. The noise grew louder and became painful. Brett stuck his fingers in his ears, closed his eyes, and dropped to his knees. He stayed that way for more than a minute until the awful noise went away.

Still kneeling on the ground and bent over, Brett felt something wet and rubbery on the back of his neck that sent shivers down his spine. Fearing an alien from the UFO had touched him, Brett leaped to his feet and cried out, "Yow!"

Seized with terror, Brett uncovered his ears, opened his eyes, and wheeled around. Then he broke out in a laugh. "Blaze, it's you!" His dog had been licking the back of Brett's neck. The boy quickly looked up in the sky in all directions, but the UFO was nowhere in sight. Unfortunately, neither was Checkers.

"Well, Blaze, I guess Checkers ran back home. I'll have to go on foot with you and the goats."

After about a half hour of walking, Brett stopped and let out a loud moan. "No! Not Checkers!" His beloved horse was lying on its side next to a large thicket. Brett rushed up to his steed and dropped to the ground so his face was next to Checkers' head.

"Thank goodness, you're breathing," he said, petting his horse. Checkers gave a couple of snorts and then tried to get up. "Easy, boy. Easy." Checkers slowly and unsteadily rose to his feet and then swayed back and forth. His eyes had the same look that Blaze had the day before—glassy, dazed, and bloodshot. One of the horse's ears had been clipped. Brett then stared at Checkers' neck. Sure enough, at the base of the mane, Brett saw a circular brown spot with an X-shaped scar. "Checkers, they got you too!"

* * *

"From now on, no one goes out on the range alone," said Dennis at the dinner table. "And when we go, we bring along our rifles."

"Dennis, is that wise?" Joan asked.

"We can't be defenseless. Besides, the kids have taken all the gun safety courses, and they're excellent target shooters. We're not going around looking to shoot space aliens, but neither are we going to be left without some sort of protection. These aliens are doing something to our animals. Who's to say they won't try to get us next?"

"I'm calling the police," Joan said. "This has gone on long enough."

About an hour later, State Highway Patrolman Cesar Melendez showed up at the ranch and heard the Hardens' eerie story. Then he examined the goats, Checkers, and Blaze. He didn't say much at first, so there was no hint whether or not he believed the Hardens.

"We're not a family of crazies," Dennis told the officer. "Somebody—or something—is doing terrible things to our animals. And we're convinced the UFO is responsible. I hope you believe us."

"Yes, Mr. Harden, I do," said Officer Melendez. "One reason is that you're not alone in seeing the UFO and in owning animals with unexplained burns and cuts.

"In the last week, I've taken four reports from ranchers who said they saw a large object—just as you described—flying over their land. The UFO hovered over a farmhouse east of here and scared a family half to death last night. This morning, the family discovered that some of their cattle had similar burns and cuts.

"Two nights ago, near Clearmont, a police officer reported that a UFO flew very low and lit up the road. It caused the engine in his car to quit and blanked out the police radio for five minutes.

"The next day, a rancher in the area reported that half a dozen of his cows had cut ears and tails and burn marks in the backs of their necks."

"What does this mean?" asked Becky.

"We don't know yet. It's the weirdest case I've ever worked on, that's for sure. In fact, I've asked for help from an independent investigator. His name is Derek Simpson, and he's a professor at the University of Wyoming. I'd like him to talk to you and look at your animals."

"Well, now we know we aren't crazy," sighed Becky. "At least we're not the only ones they're picking on."

"That gives me little comfort," said her mother.

That night, the Hardens were each in their rooms getting ready for bed when the house shook from loud zipping sounds. The family raced to their windows and looked outside. The red, whining UFO from the night before was hovering near the barn while four little round glowing white objects the size of basketballs flew out from an opening in its belly. The tiny UFOs acted as if they were dancing in the night sky. They swooped and dived as if they were putting on a show just for the Hardens, who watched with a mixture of horror and amazement. Whenever one of the objects zoomed particularly fast, it made a high-pitched shrieking sound, causing every member of the family to wince.

Her eyes locked on the UFOs, Becky asked no one in particular, "What are they?"

"Where do they come from?" wondered Brett, knowing full well no one had the answer.

"What do they want?" asked their mother.

"I don't know, but I've had about enough of this!" snapped Dennis. He grabbed his rifle and ran outside. Just as he was ready to take aim, the tiny UFOs whisked back into the mother ship and, with a house-rattling boom, the big UFO soared off into the night.

When Dennis stormed back in the house, he reached for the phone. "I'm calling the police again!" But when he picked up the phone, the line was dead. "Oh, great," he muttered. "They scare us, shake the house, and now they've messed up the phone. What could happen next?"

The Hardens found out the next day.

While checking over their herd, Becky and Brett came across two cows that acted as if they were drunk. The cows were wobbling aimlessly and had a dazed look in their eyes.

"What's the matter with them?" asked Becky. "Are they sick?"

Brett went over to one of the cows and examined her. "Becky, look at this." He pointed to a brown spot behind the base of the cow's neck. "It looks like it was burned there. The eyes are bloodshot and an ear has been cut."

Becky, who was checking the other cow, said, "The same thing has happened to this one. And there's something else. Look at the udders on your cow."

Brett did and said, "They're very red, and they have a mark on them like they were hooked up to a milking machine."

"That's exactly how the udders on this cow are. These cows have been . . ." She stopped in mid-sentence and shouted, "Brett, look! Up in the air behind you!"

The same UFO they had seen before was hovering about 300 feet (90 m) up and about a half mile (.8 km) away. "Quick," said Brett. "Let's get behind those boulders so they don't see us." The two teens quickly led their horses to the other side of the rocks and then peeked around to see what was happening.

The four basketball-sized objects from the night before drifted out from underneath the UFO and slowly floated down among a group of cows. The cattle seemed restless and mooed and walked away, but the little objects flew around them like annoying birds.

One cow took such an instant dislike that she charged one of the tiny UFOs. But it simply rose up, floated over the cow, and settled back down on the other side of her. The cow turned around and ran after

58

it again only to miss as the object rose up and then returned to its original hovering spot. After three futile charges, the cow gave up. Meanwhile, the rest of the cattle were getting increasingly agitated by the miniature UFOs as they flitted here and there among the herd.

One by one, each object selected a cow and then fired a blue beam at the back of her head. Each cow stood rigid as if she were paralyzed while the beam bored into her hide for about 30 seconds. Each cow then let out a loud moan and staggered around the ground.

"What are they doing to our cattle?" asked Becky with alarm.

"They zapped them with something," Brett replied. His eyes grew big when he saw that two of the tiny UFOs turned and headed toward him and his sister. "Uh, oh, it looks like they're coming this way to zap us! Get your rifle!"

They grabbed their weapons from the saddle pouches, loaded them, and waited as the objects drifted closer and closer to the frightened teens. Checkers and Dusty began neighing and whinnying before fleeing in a frantic gallop.

The objects headed straight for Becky and Brett, but at the last second, turned away and followed the horses. When Checkers and Dusty split and ran off in different directions, the UFOs kept tailing Dusty.

"They don't want to zap us. They want to get Dusty!" declared Becky. "Well, they're not going to get him!" She took aim with her rifle and fired. Then Brett fired his gun. But the two UFOs made a quick darting motion and avoided being hit.

"Drat! We missed them!" she said.

"Maybe so, but we scared them away."

The tiny UFOs turned away from Dusty, rose up, and circled the cattle. Then they joined the other two objects and, in single file, returned to the UFO, which then sped off out of sight, leaving in its wake another loud boom.

That night, the Hardens waited for the return of the mother ship, wondering what, if anything, would happen to them in retaliation for the kids shooting at the two small UFOs. No one dared go to sleep. But as the night wore on, there was nothing in the sky other than the innocent twinkling of the stars.

Finally, at about 1 A.M., the Hardens dozed off. But they were startled out of their sleep two hours later by the whining, whirring sound of the big UFO. Beams of yellow light suddenly flooded the house.

Brett leaped out of bed and shouted, "Everybody! Get your guns! They're here again!" Becky and her parents tumbled out of bed and ran downstairs to join Brett.

The house began to shake violently as pictures fell off the walls, lamps toppled over, and glasses crashed out of cupboards.

"We're under attack!" yelled Dennis. "Let's go out the back before the roof caves in!" They scrambled outside and hid behind a wood pile, guns poised. The UFO moved above their house until it was directly over the terrified family.

The whining sound grew louder until it hurt their ears. Then they felt an overpowering wave of static electricity that caused their hair literally to stand on end. Suddenly, Becky's rifle was ripped from her hand. So was Brett's, then their mother's gun, and their dad's weapon. Drawn by a powerful magnetic force, the weapons flew up into the air and into an opening under the UFO. Becky's hammered tin necklace pulled up against her chin and then slipped off her head and soared upward.

Finally, the whining stopped and the magnetic force disappeared. The UFO moved slowly away. But this time it didn't disappear with a thundering boom. It slowly headed back toward the other side of the ridge a mile from the ranch.

"Why do you think they did this?" asked Brett.

"They wanted to show us that they're the boss and very powerful," said Becky.

"They convinced me."

* * *

It had been a couple of hours since the latest UFO encounter. Unable to get back to sleep, Brett went out to the barn to see if Checkers was all right. When he stepped inside, he found Becky brushing Dusty.

"Couldn't get to sleep either, huh?" she asked.

"Not after what we've been through," he said.

"Brett, I've been thinking. I believe the UFO doesn't want to hurt us. Let's face it. If it wanted to harm us, it could have done it at any time."

"You're right," said Brett. "They could have zapped us easily. But all they took were our guns, and they didn't hurt us. It seems that what they really want is our animals. But what are they doing to them?"

"Who knows?" she muttered, shaking her head. "Hey, the sun's almost up. Want to go for a ride?"

They saddled their horses and ambled out toward the ridge where the UFO was last seen.

"Uh, oh, I think we have company," said Becky. A reddish color glowed from the other side of the ridge. They jumped off their horses, slowly walked to the edge, and looked down into the valley. What they saw left them speechless.

The UFO was hovering close to the ground. Bathed in bright red light were two human-like creatures and a cow. The aliens, clad in tight-fitting dark hooded uniforms, were short and extremely thin. They huddled over the cow which was lying on her side with her legs outstretched.

"What are they doing?" Becky whispered.

"I don't know. The cow isn't moving. Wow! Look what's happening now."

Slowly, the cow floated about two feet (.6 m) off the ground, turned until it was completely upside down with her legs pointed up, and remained that way in midair!

On the ground beside the aliens was a box in which they pulled out various small instruments. Holding a rod-like device that shot out a slender green laser beam, one of the aliens began operating on the cow's head.

"He's probably cutting off a piece of her ear," Becky told Brett. "And now he's doing something to her eyes."

"Look," Brett said. "The other being is cutting off a piece of her tail."

They kept watching in awe as the cow turned right-side up and floated down until her feet were back on the ground. Next, the aliens drew a blood sample from the base of her neck and, with another device, they milked her.

About five minutes later, they finished their examination. One of the aliens pointed the rod-like device and shot a laser beam at the cow's forehead. She let out a long mournful moo and staggered off.

"Thank goodness they didn't kill her," said Becky.

When the aliens repeated the procedure on three more cows, Brett said, "I'll bet those are the same cows that were zapped yesterday."

Once they were finished, the aliens floated up and into the UFO. The spacecraft then made its whining sound and took off into the sky, disappearing with another loud boom.

* * *

Later that morning the Hardens received a visit from Professor Simpson, the independent investigator, who listened intently to their story before examining the animals.

"This sounds like a classic case of alien animal research," he declared. "I've investigated over 100 similar reports in Colorado, New Mexico, Kansas, Nebraska, and Wyoming. Ranchers and farmers have discovered that their cattle and other animals have undergone mysterious surgical procedures and examinations. Almost every time, these people have seen or encountered UFOs just like you did.

"You're fortunate in one way. In many cases, animals simply have disappeared. One minute they're in a corral or pen and the next instant they're gone— and the gate is still locked. That's what happened to your goats. But at least you found them again.

"It appears that the aliens have the power to float these animals off the ground for examination or to send them up and into the craft. The aliens have some sort of device that examines the animal's eyes and causes them to become bloodshot. By studying the pupil, or center of the eye, you can learn much about the state of the entire body. The aliens seem to have a way of surgically removing small pieces of tissue from animals that causes no bleeding. The tip of the ear or the tail provide the aliens with samples that can reveal the health of the animal. So can analyzing milk from the cows."

"What about the burn marks on the back of the neck and the X-shaped scars?" asked Becky.

"The aliens appear to have some sort of laser beam that paralyzes the animal," said Dr. Simpson. "This beam probably makes them numb to any pain. The X-shaped scar might be a sign that a surgical procedure on their spine was done, or that spinal fluid was drawn from the animal for analysis."

"And the tiny UFOs?" Brett asked.

"They were probably scouts designed to select the animals."

"How many of our animals are they going to examine?"

"I doubt if the aliens will be back for some time. In the other cases, they spend only a few days before going on to another ranch or farm."

"Why would these aliens want to travel millions upon millions of miles in a UFO to examine our animals?" asked Brett.

Before Dr. Simpson could reply, Becky answered, "Maybe they're just using Earth as a science laboratory."

"Becky," said the professor, "that's about the best explanation I've heard."

THE
TIME BEING

Sixteen-year-old Jake Waterman was sitting at the kitchen table, trying to rush through his homework. He had to solve several algebra problems, learn new vocabulary words, and read a chapter in his science book. He wanted to finish as soon as possible so he could watch the last half of the basketball playoff game on TV.

But right in the middle of doing an algebra problem, Jake felt a strange and powerful urge. He had a strong desire to drive to Starved Rock, a county park about five miles from his house in Logan, Ohio. He tossed his pencil onto the table, leaned back in his chair, and scratched his curly blond hair. *Come on, Jake,* he told himself. *Clear your head. Homework first, then the basketball game.* He cracked his knuckles and turned his attention once again to the algebra problem. But his mind kept drifting back to Starved Rock.

This doesn't make sense, he thought. *I haven't been to Starved Rock in two years. Why does it keep popping into my mind? Concentrate, Jake. Now, let's see, 2X plus Y . . .*

Instead of seeing an algebra problem on the page, Jake pictured in his mind a particular place—a picnic table under a willow tree at the base of a limestone cliff next to a creek. Although he couldn't recall ever having seen this place, he had a hunch it was in Starved Rock. No matter how hard he tried, the image would not leave his mind.

"Mom," he called into the living room, "I'm going to take a break for an hour or so, okay? I just need to clear my head. I think this algebra is getting to me. Do you mind if I take the car and go for a little drive?"

"Where are you going, hon?"

"I know this sounds silly, but I thought I'd drive over to Starved Rock and . . . and . . . I don't know, just sit around or something and then come home."

"Are you meeting someone, like maybe Kara?" his mother asked suspiciously.

"No, Mom, honest, I just need to get out for a bit."

"Well, okay. It's almost eight o'clock now. Be home by nine before it gets too dark. You'll still have to finish your homework."

"I promise. Thanks, Mom."

Jake was about to go for a ride down a path that would change his life forever.

* * *

As Jake drove down the street, he kept wondering, *Why do I keep thinking about this one spot? I don't know if it even exists. I haven't been to Starved Rock in a couple of years. Why am I doing this? I've got a load of homework, and I should be studying for that vocabulary test. And I want to catch the last quarter of the basketball game. Why am I wasting my time here? Maybe I should turn around.*

But he didn't. For some reason, he just couldn't. When he arrived at Starved Rock, Jake drove slowly along the park's narrow winding road, not sure why he didn't pull off to the side at any old spot and get out. About five minutes into the park, he slammed on the brakes. "Well, I'll be," he said with amazement. Off to his left was the exact scene he had pictured in his mind—the limestone cliff, the creek, the picnic table, and the lone willow tree.

Jake walked from the car and sat down on top of the picnic table, waiting for something to happen. He had this weird feeling that something would happen, even though he didn't know what.

After listening to a concert of crickets and the hooting of an owl for a while, Jake looked at his watch. It was almost 8:30 P.M. *I guess I'd better get going. What a waste of time.* He was about to get off the picnic table, when, for no particular reason, he turned around and looked up into the sky.

He spotted a brilliant-red saucer-shaped object that grew larger and brighter as it headed toward him. At first, he thought it was a shooting star. But it was moving too slowly and didn't have a glowing tail. *What is it? Wow! Whatever it is, it's coming right at me!* Jake was set to flee, but he was so captured by this eerie sight that he stayed rooted to the table.

Within seconds, the object had descended until it was about 30 feet (9 m) off the ground and only a hundred yards (90 m) away from him. With a mixture of wonder and concern, Jake studied the bizarre object, which looked slightly larger than his car. Lights on both ends cast a red glow.

As the craft hovered silently, a bluish-white beam shot out like a spotlight and completely engulfed Jake as he sat perfectly still on the picnic table. Before he could make sense of what was happening, Jake's mind went completely blank. No thoughts. No fears. No curiosity.

In what seemed like just a second or two later, the beam turned off. The glowing red object then took off at an incredibly high rate of speed, but without making a sound, and disappeared into the sky.

"Amazing!" Jake said out loud, trying to catch his breath. "I can't believe what I just saw. That's a flying saucer! I actually saw a flying saucer!" He was so excited that he didn't realize how scared he was.

Jake jumped back into the car and headed home, anxious to tell his mother about the incredible sight he had witnessed. He burst into the house, and shouted, "Mom! Mom! You won't believe what I saw!"

"Where have you been?" snapped his mother. "You promised to be home at nine. I've been worried sick."

"But, Mom, I wasn't even gone an hour," he protested. "Why, it's only . . ." He looked at his watch and then said with surprise, "Why, it can't be ten twenty-five. Something must be wrong." He glanced at the clock on the stove. It read 10:25 too. "I don't get it. I left before eight, it takes only about 15 or 20 minutes to get to the park. It wasn't even eight-thirty when I saw the flying saucer —"

"You saw a what?"

"I know you're going to find this hard to believe, but I saw this bright red object in the sky. It came down and hovered about 300 feet (90 m) away. A beam of light shot out for a few seconds, and then the object just took off and disappeared."

"Can't you come up with an excuse better than that?" his mother said angrily.

"I'm telling you the truth, Mom."

"It's not like you to make up stories, Jake."

"I'm not making it up. It really happened. I swear to you it's true."

"How long did you watch the UFO?"

"About a minute."

"So if you saw this UFO at around eight-thirty and you watched it for a minute, what did you do for the next two hours?"

"Well, I . . . I . . ." Jake gulped. "Mom," he said with a touch of fear in his voice, "I don't remember. How could I have lost track of that much time?"

"I don't know, but to make sure you pay more attention to the time, I'm grounding you for a week."

"But I've got a date with Kara Saturday night."

"Well, now you don't. Go finish your homework."

* * *

Two weeks after the incident, Jake once again found himself trying to account for a mysterious block of time—an hour of *added* time.

Working part-time for a plumbing-supply company owned by his Uncle Bill, Jake had to pick up some fixtures in Columbus 50 miles (80 km) away and then deliver them to the warehouse before closing. He had made the round trip a couple of times before in about two and a half hours. Expecting to be back by 3 P.M., he left shortly after 12 noon and set the odometer on the company truck so the mileage could be logged in when he finished the trip.

Jake picked up the plumbing fixtures, and by 1:30 was on his way back to Logan. Traffic on the four-lane highway was fairly light at that time of day, and Jake was taking his time, not daring to go over the speed limit. He was thinking about his upcoming date with Kara when static on the radio interfered with the music on his favorite country station. He tried changing stations, but loud static drowned out the broadcasts.

Darn, the radio must be broken, he told himself. *This is going to be a boring trip home.*

It was going to be anything but boring.

About 25 miles (40 km) away from Logan, he suddenly felt a powerful urge to turn off the highway. Perplexed, Jake started arguing with himself. *Why should I stop? You need to stop and get out for a minute. This is stupid. There's no reason why I should. You've got to do it, man. Something's going to happen. No! Keep going. You've got to get these fixtures back to the warehouse. Turn off now!*

Jake couldn't help himself. He slowed down, moved to the shoulder of the highway, and turned onto a gravel road even though he knew this wasn't the right way back to the warehouse. He tried to put the brakes on, but his body wouldn't respond to what his mind ordered. As he came to an intersection with another gravel road, he tried to turn the truck around, but his arms wouldn't do what he wanted them to do. Instead, he kept on driving down the road.

No! Stop! Turn around! Get back on the highway. But it was no use. He had no choice but to give in to this strange unseen force. He drove to an abandoned gravel pit—a place he had never been to before—and stopped the truck. Just then he noticed that the truck's compass, which was attached to the rearview mirror, mysteriously was spinning wildly.

As if not in control of his will, Jake stepped out of the truck and sat down on the edge of the gravel pit. *I've got to get back to the warehouse. They need the fixtures by three o'clock. But I should be here. Why? What am I doing here? Aw, what's the use? Who cares anyway? I guess I'll wait for something to happen.*

Suddenly, a saucer-shaped craft, like the one he had seen at Starved Rock, appeared right in front of him, hovering over the gravel pit but below the rim so that Jake was looking down at it. In the daytime, the craft appeared to be made of dull stainless steel.

Jake was so astounded he sat motionless. He felt dazed for just a second, and when he blinked, the UFO was gone. Then, in what seemed like the next instant, Jake was driving down the four-lane highway on the outskirts of Logan! Startled beyond belief, he slammed on the brakes and pulled off on the side of the road.

What happened? he asked himself. *One second I'm sitting on the edge of a gravel pit 25 miles (40 km) from Logan looking at a flying saucer and the next second I'm in Logan. How can that be?* He looked at his watch. *Darn it, it's not working. Am I imagining things? How could I have forgotten driving the last 25 miles (40 km)? And what about these strange impulses that make me drive to a certain place? Are they for real? Are the flying saucers for real? If they're not, am I going crazy? That's probably it. I'm probably nuts. There's no other explanation.*

Shaking like a leaf, Jake drove the final few miles to the warehouse.

"Jake! What are you doing here?" said Tim Mason, the warehouse manager.

"I got the fixtures like you told me," Jake replied.

Tim walked to the back of the pickup truck and checked over the supplies. "Yeah, you sure did. But how could you have gone there and back so fast?"

"What are you talking about?"

"I saw you leave at about twelve-fifteen."

"So?"

"It's not even two o'clock. Jake, how did you do it? Put a rocket on the back of the truck? You must have been going over 100 miles (160 km) an hour to get back here so soon."

Jake looked at the clock on the wall. It read 1:55. "But that can't be. I left Columbus at one-thirty. It takes at least an hour to get here."

"If your uncle learns you were speeding in one of his trucks, he'll fire you for sure."

"But I swear. I wasn't speeding. As a matter of fact, I even stopped for a few minutes . . ." His voice trailed off. *The flying saucer! It's doing something crazy with time. First, I lose two hours that I can't explain. And now I gain an hour I can't explain.* Jake glanced at the odometer and was stunned by what he saw. It read 77

72

miles (124 km). *That's impossible. It should be 102 miles (164 km) round-trip. What happened to the other 25 miles (40 km)?*

* * *

Jake decided not to tell anyone about his UFO encounters. He just wanted to forget about them, hoping he would never have to deal with them again.

Unfortunately for Jake, he would face another ordeal.

A few weeks later, on a Saturday night, Jake and Kara went to visit a friend who lived out in the country. On their way back, at about 10 P.M., Jake suddenly felt the same strong impulse he had experienced twice before—that some power had control over his will. *Keep driving, Jake, keep driving,* he told himself. *Don't stop. Yes, stop. It's important. Pull over here. Do it!* Try as he might, Jake knew it was a losing battle.

"Oh, no," he moaned, breaking out in a sweat.

"Jake, what's wrong?" asked Kara.

"I don't feel so well. I need to stop for a few minutes." He pulled the car into an abandoned gas station about a mile (1.6 km) outside of town and turned off the motor and the lights. "Kara, I think something bad is going to happen to me."

"What are you talking about?"

"I don't know," he muttered, shaking his head. "I really don't know."

"Jake, you're scaring me."

"I'm sorry. That's the last thing I'd ever want to do to you. It's just —"

"What's that?" she asked, pointing out the windshield. Coming in low over the horizon behind the gas

73

station was the same saucer-shaped craft that Jake had seen twice before. As it did the first night, the UFO had a red glow to it.

"It must be a blimp," said Kara. "I'll bet that's what it is, because it looks like it has its message lights on. Wait a second, that's strange." Her voice began to rise in fear. "That's no blimp. It's . . . it's . . ."

"It's come back again!" Jake cried.

Everything went dark for what seemed like a split second. Then the two were staring at each other.

"What happened?" asked Kara. "I feel kind of woozy."

"Me too."

"It's gone. Was that a UFO?"

"Stay here," said Jake. "Let me check it out. I'll be right back."

"No way. I'm coming with you."

The two of them walked cautiously along the side of the gas station. Then with their hearts pounding, they peeked around the back corner, not knowing what to expect. "Whew!" said Jake. "There's nothing here."

As they walked back to the car, Kara asked, "What did you mean in the car when you said 'it's come back again'?"

"Oh, um," Jake fumbled for the words, trying to buy time before deciding whether or not to tell her about his UFO encounters. Finally, he made up his mind. "Kara, I'm going to tell you something really outrageous, but I don't want you to laugh at me, okay?"

She nodded.

"What we saw definitely was a UFO. And I've seen it twice before—once at Starved Rock and again on my way back from Columbus."

"Why didn't you tell me before?"

"I thought you'd think I was weird or something."

"Don't be silly. I believe in UFOs. Why should we humans think we have the whole universe to ourselves?"

"Yeah, I guess you're right."

Jake started the car and put on the radio. "Our request lines will be open until midnight," said the disc jockey. "So if you have a song you want dedicated to your sweetheart, you've got only five more minutes."

Jake's heart sank. "Did he say it's almost midnight?"

"That's not right," said Kara. She looked at her watch and gasped. "It's eleven fifty-five! What happened to the time? It was only ten o'clock when we stopped, and we weren't here more than 15 minutes. Now it's nearly midnight—and I was supposed to be home an hour ago! Jake, we're in trouble. My parents are going to kill me—and you too."

"I'm so sorry I got you involved," said Jake. Then, pounding the steering wheel, he looked up and shouted, "This has got to stop! I can't stand it anymore!"

"What are you talking about?"

"Kara, I haven't told you the whole story. So here goes." He then told her about the strange feelings, the UFO incidents at Starved Rock and the gravel pit, and the altering of time. "And now this," he said. "At first, I thought I was losing my mind. But now it's happened to you—at least you saw the UFO and you've experienced missing time. I feel so badly that I got you into this."

"If what you say is true, then what happened between ten-fifteen and midnight?" she asked.

"I don't know."

"I'm getting goose bumps," Kara said. "I've read where people claim they were taken by aliens and examined. Later, when the people were returned, their memories of the experience were wiped out."

"Then how did they know they were taken aboard?"

"They were hypnotized and able to recall all the things that were hidden in their memory."

"Do you think we have things hidden in our memory?" asked Jake.

* * *

"Jake," said Kara excitedly over the phone a week later. "Something incredible has happened."

"Yeah, your folks have returned your phone privileges and you're no longer grounded, right?"

"That too," she replied. "But what I'm about to tell you is going to knock your socks off. It's so . . . so unbelievable!"

"All right already. Tell me."

"My sister Sally knows a professor at Ohio State, Dr. Ralph Furman, who investigates UFO cases. He uses what's called hypnotic regression to get people who have seen UFOs to remember things about their experiences. Anyway, he hypnotized me to see what happened about that missing time."

"So, did you meet any aliens?"

"Not exactly. But while I was under hypnosis, I recalled that we were at the gas station when we spotted the UFO. Now here's where it gets amazing. I saw a strange man walking toward us. He was about 4 feet (1.2 m) tall, wore green overalls, and a skull cap, and had extremely thin arms and legs. Jake, he wasn't human! He came over to us and I started screaming.

Then I couldn't remember anything more under hypnosis.

"Dr. Furman believes the alien was after you! He thinks the aliens have talked to you or examined you before and then made you forget. That could explain the other two time lapses you experienced. Dr. Furman wants to hypnotize you. Will you do it?"

"If it will prove I'm not crazy, let's do it."

The next day, while sitting in a chair, Jake was hypnotically regressed by Dr. Furman.

"Let's go back a few weeks," said the hypnotist. "You're sitting on the picnic table at Starved Rock, and you see a red object hovering nearby. What happens?"

"A beam of light shoots out and I'm blinded," Jake recalled. "I feel like I'm floating and moving toward this spaceship. It's like I'm lifted up, but there's nothing holding me. Now I'm in a round white room. A tall person is there, but he's not like a human. He's over six feet (1.8 m) tall, has a head like E.T., and big eyes. He just stares in my eyes and touches my forehead."

"How do you feel?" asked Dr. Furman.

"I'm not scared. I'm trying to relax, but it's not easy. I don't think he wants to hurt me."

"Does he say anything to you?"

"Not the way humans talk. It's just a feeling, like he's taken over my mind and can put thoughts in my head."

"What are the thoughts?" asked Dr. Furman.

"That they won't harm me. That they're just going to do a little examination, but it won't hurt me and then they'll let me go. I can't think of anything but those eyes. They overpower me. How do they do that? His gaze goes right inside me, and I can't stop looking at him. My eyes are wide open, but my mind is sort of gone. I have no will. I can't fight it . . ."

"What happens next?" asked Dr. Furman.

"They take me into another room, like an examining room but . . . I can't remember. I'm not supposed to remember."

"Okay, let's move on to two weeks later. You're driving the pickup truck back from Columbus."

"I'm at a gravel pit and I can't figure out why," Jake recalled. "Then I see the UFO hover overhead and that same beam of light shoots out. Now a different alien is sitting beside me. He's much smaller than the one I met the first time. But he's kind of the same, with skinny arms and legs. He says, 'See how easily we made you come to this place? In the future, when you're supposed to go to a certain place, you'll be made to go there. Don't worry about it, because there's nothing you can do. Just accept it.'

"I ask him if this is all a joke or if I'm going crazy. He says it's real. He says not to doubt them because they're so powerful. They can do things we can only dream about. He says to prove it, he will play with time. I ask him what that means, and he says I'll find out."

"What happens next?" asked Dr. Furman.

"Just like that, I'm driving on the highway on the outskirts of town and I can't figure out why."

"Okay, let's go to the night you and Kara parked by the gas station," said the hypnotist. "What happens after you both see the UFO?"

"Kara sees someone walking toward us. He's about four feet (1.2 m) tall, dressed in a tight dark green suit, has a big head and long thin arms. He looks like the alien I saw at the gravel pit. Kara says, 'Jake, I'm so scared. He doesn't look real, like a real human. Let's get out of here! Go! Go!'

"I see him, but I don't respond. I don't have the will to do anything. She leans over and tries to start the ignition herself, but the car's engine won't turn over. She screams, 'Let's run for it!' and reaches for the door. But then her arms and legs go limp, and she slumps back in her seat. Her eyes remain open, but she can't move or speak. She looks like she's in a hypnotic trance.

"I leave with the alien, but I don't want to go. I don't want to leave Kara alone. I say, 'Please don't let anything happen to her. She's going to be so scared when she wakes up and I'm not there for her.'

"He takes me around to the back of the gas station where there are four more aliens standing near the flying saucer, which is hovering close by. I ask if they're going to take me away. They say not to worry, that nothing bad will happen. I'm not scared for me, but I'm scared for Kara. They tell me she's not going to remember anything. We're walking underneath the spaceship. And now we're inside and I'm lying on a table.

"I ask, 'Why are you doing this to me?' This tall alien says, 'Empty your mind. Don't think about anything.'

"I say, 'How can I not think about anything? There's so much going on.' And he keeps repeating, 'Empty your mind. Let it all go away.' Soon I feel nothing, like I'm floating with no thoughts in my head."

Jake paused and wrinkled his forehead, trying hard to recall more details under hypnosis. Finally, he told

Dr. Furman, "They won't let me remember anymore."

"What's the next thing you remember?" asked the hypnotist.

"I'm in the car, and Kara and I are talking about the UFO. We realize it's almost midnight when we thought it should be around 10:15."

When Jake came out of the hypnosis session, he looked Dr. Furman in the eye and said, "So tell, me, Doc, am I crazy or what?"

"I don't think you're crazy," replied Dr. Furman. "What you've described is similar to what hundreds of other sincere, normal people of all ages have recalled under hypnosis. Some have reported an unexplained loss of time or, in rare cases such as yours, a strange gain of time. These aliens have incredible powers to control our minds and alter time. How they use these powers and for what reason, I don't know."

Fortunately for Jake, he has never experienced another UFO encounter—at least, none that he can remember.

THE UFO TEARDROPS

Shortly before bedtime, 14-year-old Danni Larkin was walking her yellow Labrador retriever Max along the gravel road that led to her house in the South Carolina low country. It was a picture-perfect spring evening. A late afternoon shower had left everything smelling fresh and clean. The aroma from night-blooming jasmine sweetened the air.

Danni enjoyed listening to the chirping, croaking music from Mother Nature. The crickets, night warblers, and tree frogs seemed especially loud and in good form.

As Danni gazed up in the sky, she saw what she thought was the planet Jupiter shining brightly below the lower point of the crescent-shaped moon. But just as she was about to take her eyes off the greenish-white twinkle in the sky, "Jupiter" moved. Danni stopped and stared as it drifted slowly under the moon. She told herself, *It must be a plane or maybe a satellite or . . . Wow!* The object suddenly dove in an arc and disappeared behind the trees. *That's no satellite. I wonder what it was.*

Danni continued walking toward home when Max began to whimper. His ears flopped down and his tail slipped between his legs.

"What's wrong, boy? Are you all right?" Danni looked around and didn't see anything. "Is there a wild animal nearby? Is that what's scaring you?"

It was then she noticed something that made her feel slightly uncomfortable. The chirping, croaking, and warbling had stopped. The night was deathly silent, so quiet she could hear Max's paws stepping on the gravel.

"Everything sure hushed up all of a sudden," she told Max, as she pulled her open, button-down sweater a little tighter around her. "Come on, Max, let's walk a little faster."

When Danni looked down at him, she noticed a blue light reflecting off a puddle. She glanced up and saw a beam of blue light about 300 feet (90 m) away shining down through the trees in her backyard near the family's 10-foot- (3-m-) tall bird feeder. But a second later, the beam was gone.

"What do you suppose that was, Max?" asked Danni, breaking out in a trot. Max kept whimpering and skulking lower to the ground as he lagged farther behind her.

When she finally reached the clearing in her backyard, Danni looked up and saw the bright green object she earlier had mistaken for Jupiter. It was much closer, although it was moving away at a remarkable speed.

"Wasn't that strange, Max?" asked Danni. She turned around but couldn't find her dog anywhere. "Max? Max?

Where are you? Come here, boy." Max always came when he was called. But this time, he didn't. He let out a frightened bark instead. Danni followed the sound of his bark and found him hiding under the family car.

"Come on out, silly. It's okay." She spent a couple of minutes before finally coaxing him out. Even so, Max ran straight to the house and furiously pawed on the door to be let in. While Max scooted under a chair, Danni told her parents about the blue light and the UFO. However, they hadn't seen or heard anything unusual.

The next morning at breakfast, Danni looked outside, expecting to see the mourning doves and cardinals crowding around the bird feeder for their daily feast. "Something's wrong," she told her father, Tom. "The ground next to the bird feeder looks burned. And there's not a single bird in sight."

They went out to inspect the lawn. A teardrop-shaped area—rounded on one side and pointed on the other—about five feet (1.5 m) long and three feet (.9 m) wide was completely black. The grass inside the area had died.

"It looks like somebody poured gasoline on the lawn and burned it," said Tom. "But there's no evidence of any fire touching the bird feeder." He got down on his hands and knees and sniffed the blackened ground. "And there's no smell of smoke or gasoline. Lightning maybe?"

"I think it has something to do with that blue light I saw last night—and it wasn't lightning," said Danni. "Max was acting real strange too, like he was afraid of it. Look at him, he's still acting scared. Come here, boy, come to Danni." Max took a step toward her and then backed up. He wanted to obey her, but he just couldn't do it. He whined and walked around the outside of the blackened area, refusing to put one paw inside it.

Over the next few days, Danni noticed that no bird would land on the feeder even though it was full of birdseed. The squirrels wouldn't go near it. And Max stayed far away whenever he was in the backyard.

* * *

As an amateur photographer, Danni loved taking pictures for the school paper and the yearbook. Friends nicknamed her "Snapper" because she was always snapping photos at school, parties, and wherever kids hung out.

At twilight, three days after she first spotted the UFO, Danni and Max were walking along a path that took them by the edge of Willow Lake, a half-mile (.8 km) from her house. Danni brought her camera along, planning to take pictures of what she hoped would be a spectacular sunset.

During their walk, Max began to whine again and refused to go any farther. "What's the matter, boy?"

The dog gave a frightened bark and tucked his tail between his legs. When Danni bent down to pet her trembling dog, she noticed his ears were cocked. "What do you hear, Max?"

She stood up and gazed at the calm lake. The sun was setting, triggering a beautiful, partly cloudy sky of golds, purples, and pinks. "The light is perfect, Max," said Danni. She snapped a couple of photos. "These are going to look so good."

She put the camera up to her eye again and was about to snap a photo when a green-glowing object moved across her field of vision. She put her camera down and looked up at the sky. The craft, shaped like an overturned bowl about the size of a garage, hovered over the forest preserve that butted up against the lake. "Look at that! It's a UFO!"

Quickly, Danni took a photo of it seconds before it zoomed out of sight. She looked around to see if anyone else was by the lake who might have witnessed the UFO, but she was alone.

"It had to be a UFO, Max! It just had to be. And I've got a picture of it. This is great. This is fantastic. This is front-page news!" She gulped and added in a less thrilled voice, "This is scary." Her heart started pounding with excitement. "But I can't wait to get this developed."

Clutching her camera, Danni kept looking at the sky, hoping to get one more shot of the object. "There it is again!" She put the camera to her eye, focused, and then . . .

A laser-like beam of blue light shot out of the UFO and hit a few yards in front of her on the rock-strewn, sandy bank of the lake. Startled and momentarily blinded by the beam, Danni dropped her camera. It smashed onto a large rock, cracked open, and then plopped into the water.

"Oh, no! My camera!" Danni shouted in dismay. "It's busted. There goes my great UFO shot."

Max didn't hear a word she said. He had taken off in a mad dash when the blue beam struck the bank.

Danni stomped on the ground, muttering over her bad luck, and walked down to the bank where she began picking up pieces of her camera. When she reached for the broken lens, it felt warm to the touch. She stood up and said out loud, "What in the world . . ."

She noticed that the spot where the blue beam had struck now looked like a large piece of glass. After examining the spot carefully, Danni shuddered. It was the same size and shape as the mysterious black, pointed teardrop on her backyard lawn.

Danni rushed home, told her father what had happened, and brought him back to look at the lakeside teardrop. "It definitely was under intense heat," he told her. "When sand is heated at a tremendous temperature, it turns to glass. Whatever did this cooked the sand. I'm going to call the authorities."

* * *

That night, Danni baby-sat for 8-year-old Shannon Harper at the little girl's farm two miles (3.2 km) away. Before putting Shannon to bed, Danni agreed to play with her on the backyard monkey bars.

As they were hanging upside down from their knees on the bar, Shannon said, "Wouldn't it be cool to live millions of years ago when the dinosaurs were here?"

"Yeah, you could ride one to school."

"And we could train raptors to act as our guard dogs and . . ." Suddenly the monkey bars began to vibrate. "Hey, did you feel that?" asked Shannon.

Danni felt the top bar vibrating in the crook behind the back of her legs. "It almost tickles."

The chains on the swing set next to the monkey bars began to rattle, and the swings started swaying back and forth on their own.

"What's going on?" asked Shannon. Before Danni could answer, they both yelled, "Look!" Still hanging by their knees, the girls stared into the sky at a green-glowing craft as it slowly moved over them. The startled girls flipped off the monkey bars and landed on their feet. The object, which was as big as a house, continued silently by. Then the craft rocketed out of sight without making a sound or leaving any kind of vapor trail.

"What was that?" Shannon asked fearfully.

Not wanting to alarm her, Danni told a white lie. "Oh, it was nothing. They're probably testing a new kind of plane. Come on, let's go inside." Outwardly calm, Danni felt a touch of fear about seeing the UFO for the third time.

A few hours later, the Harpers returned home. "Everything go okay, Danni?" Mrs. Harper asked.

Danni wanted to tell them about the UFO but decided against it. *They might not believe me, and then they won't want me to sit for Shannon anymore,* she thought. "No problem," Danni replied. "Shannon was an angel as usual."

Danni hopped into Mr. Harper's car for the ride home. About a mile (1.6 km) down the road, Danni gasped, "Look Mr. Harper, over to the left." It was the UFO—and it was heading right toward them.

"Well, I'll be," said Mr. Harper. "I've never seen anything like it."

Suddenly, the car's headlights went out. Then the radio, the dashboard lights, and finally the engine died. The car coasted to a stop. "What happened to my car?" he moaned. Meanwhile, the UFO slowed down and hovered about 50 feet (15 m) above the road in front of them. "What am I staring at?" asked Mr. Harper.

Danni gulped and in a shaky voice replied, "It's a UFO. And I'm pretty sure I've seen it before. It shoots out a blue beam—" Suddenly a shaft of blue light shined on the road for a couple of seconds and turned off. "Just like that!"

Then the UFO flew up and away. Clutching the steering wheel with both hands, Mr. Harper stared out the windshield with his mouth wide open, not saying a word.

"Mr. Harper, are you all right?" asked Danni.

"Huh? Oh, yeah," he said, shaking his head in awe. "I'm just stunned at what I saw. I've heard about UFOs and read about them, but I've never seen one in person—until now."

He turned the ignition key, and the car started right up. The headlights, dashboard lights, and radio came back on too. As the car slowly rolled ahead, the headlights shined on the spot where the blue beam had hit. "Stop the car, Mr. Harper," Danni said.

He did, and they cautiously stepped out and examined the country highway. A large, pointed black teardrop had been burned into the asphalt. It was the exact same size and shape as the other two teardrops in the ground that Danni had discovered.

* * *

The next morning, after a call from Danni's father, Sheriff Turner Reed examined the three teardrops. "I don't have any idea what caused these burns," he told the Larkins afterwards. "At first I thought maybe some kids did it as a prank. But my office has received six other calls from people who claim they saw a strange object in the sky. Now, after hearing what Danni and Jeb Harper saw, well, anything is possible. Including a UFO. Quite frankly, this is out of my league."

Danni's father contacted a UFO investigator who was due to arrive in the area in a couple of days. But

Danni couldn't wait that long. She decided to do her own investigating.

Starting in her own backyard, she studied the teardrop from every angle. *I wonder if the shape means anything,* she thought. *What could it be? A message? A symbol? What?* Nothing clicked in her mind.

She bicycled over to the lake and examined the spot on the bank struck by the blue beam. The teardrop was perfectly formed, as if a furnace had molded the glass. The sand only an inch (2.5 cm) away from the edge of the teardrop looked like it had not been affected by the heat.

Danni then rode her bike to the pointed teardrop in the road. Again, she walked around the burned mark several times. She even climbed a tall roadside tree to get a different view of it, hoping that would provide her with a clue. But it didn't.

Feeling defeated, Danni climbed down the tree and sat in the shade against the trunk. *There has to be a meaning to all this,* she told herself. *There just has to be.* Deep in thought, she stared off in the distance and saw a weather vane on top of a barn turning in the wind. Then she reached down and picked up a tall blade of grass to chew. *Hey, wait a second!* She looked again at the weather vane, which was a rusted metal bird. *That's shaped sort of like a teardrop. Maybe, just maybe . . .* She scrambled to her feet, ran over to the teardrop in the road, and said, "I think I've got it figured out!"

Danni sprinted home on her bike, grabbed a compass, and raced out to the backyard. She stood over the point of the blackened teardrop on her lawn. It was aiming northwest. Then she dashed over to the lake and discovered the teardrop was aiming due west. Finally, she returned to the country-road teardrop and determined that it was pointing south-southeast.

I'm on to something here, I can feel it! thought Danni as she biked swiftly back home. She rummaged around the house until she pulled out a map of the county. Using her compass and a ruler, she drew a line from her house to the northwest. Then she drew a line due west from the lake and another south-southeast from the teardrop in the road. The three lines met at one spot—directly over a steep wooded area known as Stark Hill, the highest spot in the county. Danni didn't know what, if anything, it meant. But she was convinced that Stark Hill was somehow involved with the UFO and the teardrop markings.

She wanted to share her discovery with her parents, but they weren't home. She called two of her best friends, only to find they couldn't get away. *I can't wait. I'm going out there myself. It's not that far. It will take me less than an hour to get there.*

Leaving Max behind, Danni biked to Stark Hill. She parked her bicycle against a tree and headed into the woods, wondering what she would find. A sense of fear crept over her, and she began having second thoughts. *Maybe it isn't such a good idea to come out here alone. I don't even know what I'm looking for. What if I bump into an alien? Will I scream? Will I freak out? Will it be friendly or dangerous? Why did I do this? Maybe I should turn around.* But Danni didn't. She kept weaving her way through the trees, slowly and carefully. She was looking for something, but she didn't know what.

What's that up ahead? Between shafts of sunlight and the dark shadows of trees, she caught a glimpse of a bright blue light. Her heart skipped a beat. Fighting the urge to turn around, Danni crept forward. Like a squirrel, Danni skittered from the base of one tree trunk to another, never taking her eyes off the blue light. She then stepped into a small clearing and stopped.

There on the ground sat a black box no bigger than a TV, giving off a dazzling ray of blue light that shot up about five feet (1.5 m). Danni felt scared and wanted to turn and run. But an overpowering curiosity caused her to step closer to the box. *Why am I going toward the box? I really should go home now.*

Ever so cautiously, Danni walked up to the box. It was issuing a soft buzzing sound that reminded her of a small electric motor. She kneeled down and gave it a quick poke with her index finger.

"It's all right. You can touch it."

Danni let out a scream and leaped to her feet. She turned in a complete circle, looking for the source of the voice. But she didn't see a soul. "Who said that?" she asked, still moving in a circle, her eyes wildly scanning the woods for signs of life. "Where are you?"

"I'm right here—in a manner of speaking." Danni turned around and screamed again. The voice was coming from the black box.

Trying to crack a smile, Danni asked warily, "What is this, some kind of joke? Am I being videotaped for a TV show?"

"No, I can assure you it's nothing like that."

Suddenly, the blue beam atop the box turned into a vivid purple that swirled until the head of a human-like being appeared and floated above the box. Danni gasped and jumped back. The head was large and oblong with gray-brown skin and huge black eyes that shimmered in the shadows. The face had holes for ears and a nose. The mouth was tiny and barely moved, although the voice was strong.

"Don't be alarmed," said the head. "What you are looking at is a live hologram—something like a three-dimensional television broadcast."

"Are you from the UFO?" asked the petrified teen.

"Yes. What is your name?"

"Danni, Danni Larkin."

"I assume you are afraid, but you need not be."

"Well, it's not every day I talk to an alien."

"I am pleased you found me."

"Why do I get the feeling you were expecting me?" she said.

"You showed great reasoning and intelligence to find me."

"You mean all this was a test to see if I could figure out what those pointed teardrops meant? Why? And why me?"

"Questions, questions, questions. What you need to know will be revealed to you in due time."

"Can't you tell me who you are or where you come from or why you're here?"

"In due time."

"Well, how about giving me some really stupendous information that will help the human race? You know, like a cure for cancer, or ways to travel back in time, or how to make us live hundreds of years."

"We are not miracle makers."

"Can you tell me *anything?*"

The holographic head faded away, replaced by a three-dimensional scene that Danni instantly recognized as our solar system. The scene shifted to the Milky Way—a galaxy made up of many solar systems, including our own. Then it switched to a different solar system on the other side of the Milky Way before zeroing in on a red planet.

Danni watched spellbound as the hologram took her on a one-minute whirlwind aerial view of the planet— an orange sky with two red suns, fiery volcanos, blue jungles, pink oceans, and cities with blinding white buildings that had curves rather than sharp corners.

And then the hologram disappeared.

"That was neat," said Danni, somewhat disappointed that it went so fast. "Is there any more?" She waited for a response from the alien, but there was none. "Hello? Hello? Are you there?"

After a couple of minutes of silence, Danni started to walk away. *The box,* she thought. *Take the box home. It would be the greatest discovery ever. Maybe the alien will talk with our world leaders. And I'll be famous because I'm the one who found it.* Danni turned and moaned. "Oh, no! It's gone!" She dropped to her knees where the box had been and dug around the ground, but found nothing.

Disappointed yet thrilled by the encounter, she walked back to her bicycle. *Gee, I'd sure like to visit that planet some time,* she told herself.

And then in her head, she heard the alien's voice say, "Perhaps you will, Danni, perhaps you will."

TERROR
IN THE
OUTBACK

I want them to go away," sobbed Chloe Ferguson. "To leave us alone. To let us live in peace."

The 17-year-old fell to her knees in the middle of the living room and sobbed, pounding the floor with her fists. "I can't take this anymore. Look what they've done to our family."

With a trembling hand, she pointed to her 15-year-old brother Luther, his hair singed, and his arms and legs laced with scratches . . . then to her 12-year-old sister Bethany, whose eyes were red from sleepless nights of terror . . . and finally to her 14-year-old brother Johnny, who sat dazed from the horrors he had witnessed.

"We have to leave, or our lives will be ruined forever!"

* * *

Living in the outback of Australia wasn't easy for the Ferguson family. The dust storms, the loneliness, the hard-scrabble life where nature can often seem to be cruel.

Although life was tough for the Fergusons, nothing could have prepared them for the horror they were about to face. It all began when the family suffered its first heart-stopping crisis. Luther was missing.

The tall redhead had taken his trail bike and pedaled the 12 miles (19 km) into town for a few supplies for his family. Luther bought the groceries and was last seen heading home by taking a shortcut through the outback that sliced two miles (3.2 km) off the trip.

His mother, Matilda, wasn't too worried when he failed to show up by 4 P.M. But as dinner time neared, she and her husband James became more concerned. James headed out in his pickup truck and searched for his son, but couldn't find any sign of him or the bike by nightfall.

The next day, a search party made up of towns-people combed the area. To the Fergusons' alarm, they found Luther's bike about four miles (6 km) from the house. But there was no trace of the teen.

"That's strange," said a police officer as he examined the bicycle. The rubber hand grips and pedals were twisted and bent as if they had been under intense heat. The bicycle seat was blistered and smelled of smoke. "The ground looks like it's been burned," said the officer. The soil in an area about the size of a football field had a distinctly different color and feel—similar to crushed charcoal—than the red dusty ground throughout the rest of the region. "Something very hot caused this—but what?"

"I don't know," said James. "The only question I want answered right now is, where is my son?"

Two more days went by without a clue to Luther's fate. But then late in the afternoon on the fourth day, Cliff Barnett, a rancher who was part of the search party, spotted a young redheaded man in jeans and a T-shirt lying in a gully about a mile (1.6 km) from where the bike had been found.

"Luther!" shouted Barnett. "It's you! You're alive!"

Luther didn't say a word. His eyes seemed like they were looking off in the distance, and not focused on his rescuer.

"Are you hurt?" Barnett asked. "Are you okay?"

Luther remained in a zombie-like trance. Checking Luther for injuries, the rancher saw that the teen's hair was burned, and his arms had strange scratches and marks on them. "Luther, can you talk? Can you tell me what happened?"

The boy didn't shake or nod his head. He remained silent. Barnett pulled the teen to his feet, but the boy's legs were so weak that they buckled, and he fell to the ground. Barnett picked him up, laid him across his horse, walked to the nearest highway two miles (3.2 km) away, and summoned help.

Luther was taken to the local hospital where he was examined by Dr. Truman Taylor. "His vital signs are fine," the physician told the Fergusons, who had rushed to the waiting room. "No broken bones or internal injuries. He acts like there's some brain damage, but I can't find any. He's completely mute—won't say a word. And he hardly moves a muscle even though it appears he's not physically paralyzed.

Clearly, something traumatic happened to him, judging by the scratches, burned hair, and his inability to communicate.

"It's a very strange case, because I can't find anything physically wrong with him. He's what I call a locked-in patient. He's awake and his eyes are open, but they're in a fixed stare. He doesn't respond to anything you say. I asked him to lift his hand and he just wouldn't move. Not even to blink his eyes.

"I tried to move his arms and legs, but couldn't. I pricked them with a sharp pin to test his sensitivities, but he showed no reaction at all. No pain anywhere. We have him on IVs because he won't eat or drink anything. But at least he's breathing well and he's not in a coma."

"Then what's the matter with him?" asked Matilda.

"My guess is that something terrible has scared him so much it's put him in a trance," the doctor replied.

"But what could have happened to him?" asked Matilda.

The family took shifts, sitting by Luther's bedside around the clock, talking to him and comforting him, urging him to speak. But all he did was stare straight ahead. Finally, after three days in the hospital, Luther mumbled his first words to his sister Chloe.

"Paper," he whispered. "Pencil."

"Oh, thank goodness you're talking!" she cried out. Chloe rushed to the nurse's station and brought back paper and pencil. "Tell me what happened, Luther. Tell me."

Barely able to hold the pencil, he drew a crude sketch of a disc-shaped object hovering over the desert. Then he drew another picture of a stick figure on a bicycle.

"That's you, right?" said Chloe. "But what's the first drawing mean?"

Luther scrawled three letters that sent goose bumps up and down Chloe's arms. "UFO."

"Are you saying you were taken aboard a UFO?"

Luther nodded, dropped the pencil and paper, turned his head toward his sister, and cried. Chloe held his trembling hand. "It's okay," she said soothingly. "It's over now." Meanwhile, her head was spinning, wondering whether her brother was hallucinating or telling the truth.

* * *

"You can tell us what happened," said Matilda, as she sat next to her son's hospital bed later that day.

Luther gazed at the other members of his family who were standing in the room. Each one encouraged him to explain what had happened.

"Promise me you won't think I'm crazy, okay?" he said haltingly in a weak voice. "It's hard to think about it, let alone talk about it." He took a few breaths and said, "I was pedaling home when I heard a loud boom. I looked up and saw a bright light—brighter than the sun. It hurt my eyes, and I could look at it only for a moment.

"Suddenly, I felt an intense heat. I fell flat on my back on the ground. I couldn't move and I didn't know why. I was paralyzed and scared out of my wits. I heard a whooshing sound. This bright object—it was bigger than a helicopter—hovered directly over me. Then I began to rise in the air by myself. Some force was pulling me up, yet nothing was touching me. I was completely helpless.

"I stared at the object again and it wasn't so bright anymore. It was oval-shaped, and there was an opening in the bottom. I went inside it. Then the opening closed, and I fell on the floor, but not hard.

"I was lying on my back, still paralyzed, but I could look around. There were two little people inside, but they weren't human. They were about three feet (.9 m) tall and seemed real skinny—they had arms and legs like monkeys, but without the hair. I couldn't see their faces or skin because they were dressed in long hoods and wore helmets with mirrored glass.

"They didn't seem to pay any attention to me at first. They talked to each other in a language I can't even describe. Their voices were loud but they weren't like human sounds.

"Then they turned toward me, and I was floated onto a smooth, flat table. I was still paralyzed. Then they started to cut me on my arms and legs. I wanted to scream but nothing came out of my mouth. And then I blanked out.

"The next thing I knew I was lying in a gully, and Mr. Barnett was calling out to me. I wanted to shout back. I tried to get up and move. But I couldn't do anything. During my first few days in the hospital, I wanted to respond to you and the doctors. But I felt trapped inside my body. I simply couldn't say or do anything until now."

The room fell silent as each family member tried to digest this astonishing tale. There was no reason to doubt him. What little physical evidence they had matched his incredible story—the burned rubber from the bike, the charred earth, his singed hair, the cuts on his arms and legs, and his mental condition.

"Well," said Matilda, breaking the uneasy silence. "You're with us now. You're safe."

"No, Mom, we're not safe," he replied with tears welling in his eyes. "They're going to come back. I know it."

* * *

Luther was discharged from the hospital four days later, but it took him several more weeks until he felt ready to go on with his life. Although every day he wondered if he would be kidnapped again, he was able to do his chores and go back to school.

What helped him, besides the support of his family, was that there were no new reports of any UFO sightings in the area. However, several people had claimed they saw strange bright lights in the sky in the days before his abduction.

About two months after Luther's frightening ordeal, James and Matilda were driving home from town about 8 P.M. on a lonely stretch of road when they spotted two glowing white balls of light in the sky. Suddenly, one of the objects veered off and headed in the direction of their house about nine miles (14 km) away. But the other ball kept aiming straight for their car.

"What in the world is that?" asked James. Staring at the UFO, he paid no attention to the road. They were heading for a ditch when Matilda grabbed the steering wheel and jerked the car back onto the highway.

By now the object was directly overhead and flooded the area with a blinding yellow light. Just then, the car's engine conked out and the car rolled to a stop.

"It's a spaceship, James!" Matilda cried. "What are we going to do?"

"Let's make a run for it!" He grabbed her hand, opened the driver's side door and jumped out, yanking her with him. They immediately were caught in a hot dusty whirlwind from which they could not escape.

Meanwhile, back home, Chloe, Bethany, and Johnny were kicking a soccer ball back and forth about 50 yards (46 m) from the house when Bethany saw a brilliant white light low in the horizon. It moved with incredible speed, angling toward the ground.

Pointing out the object to the others, Bethany shouted, "It's coming right at us!"

"It's a UFO!" yelled Johnny. "Get in the house!"

The object was so bright that the ground lit up. As the three Ferguson children scrambled toward the house, Bethany's sandal strap broke, and she fell in a heap, spraining her ankle. Johnny turned around and saw his younger sister sprawled on the ground. He also saw that the UFO was closing in on her.

Not realizing her little sister was in trouble, Chloe kept running toward the house. Johnny, however, raced back to Bethany, helped her up, and together they tried to make a mad dash for safety. But it was too late. A beam of yellow light zeroed in on them, and instantly they felt a tingling sensation throughout their bodies.

A tremendously hot wind swirled around them before a strange force pulled them about four feet (1.2 m) off the ground. "I can't touch the ground!" cried Johnny. "What's happening to us?" He could see the stark terror in Bethany's eyes and hear her shrieking, "Help me! Help me!"

Both terrified kids were pumping their arms and legs in a futile effort to free themselves. But all they were doing was running on air. *This can't be real,* Johnny told himself. *I don't want to die! I don't want to die!* The hot wind continued to spin around both of them as they flailed their arms like drowning victims.

When Chloe reached the front door, she turned around and screamed at the sight. Then she burst inside the house and yelled at the top of her lungs, "Luther, the UFO! It's outside—and it's got Johnny and Bethany!"

Luther rushed to the window and cried out with alarm when he saw the blinding-bright object hovering over Johnny and Bethany, who were still struggling in midair. The horrible sight caused Luther to slump to the floor in shock.

Abruptly, the hot swirling wind underneath the UFO stopped, and Johnny and Bethany tumbled to the ground. Moments later, the craft gradually rose about 200 feet (60 m) into the air and then zoomed out of sight.

The two teens remained crumpled on the ground, too dazed to move or speak. Finally, Johnny managed to blurt out, "Bethany . . . are . . . you . . . all right?" He crawled over to her as she slowly sat up. She tried to talk, but all she could do was sob hysterically.

With Chloe by his side, Luther recovered from his own emotional jolt and raced outside. Luther assisted Johnny while Chloe helped pick up Bethany and led them back into the house. Trembling with fear and shock, Bethany and Johnny sat and cried, unable to blurt out one complete sentence for nearly half an hour. Luther and Chloe examined them for any injuries but didn't find any, other than their hair had been singed.

When they regained their composure, Bethany asked, "Why are they doing this to us? What do they want?"

"I wish I knew," said Luther.

"Maybe we should get out of here right now," Chloe said, "before it comes back."

"Good idea," said Luther.

"What about Mom and Dad?" asked Bethany.

"We'll leave them a note. Let's hope we'll find them on the road."

"First, let me call the police and tell them what's going on," Johnny said. He picked up the phone and his heart sank. "The line is dead."

"Come on, let's go before it's too late," Luther urged.

The Ferguson kids piled into their dad's old pickup truck. But when Chloe turned the ignition switch, the engine refused to start. "It's that dumb starter."

"No it's not," said Luther. "It's that UFO."

"What are we going to do now?" Chloe asked.

"There's not much we can do but stay inside and lock the doors."

When they returned to the house, Bethany began to whimper. "I wish Mom and Dad were home. Where are they? You don't suppose the spacemen got them, do you?"

None of the others wanted to answer her. They didn't dare say out loud what they already feared— that their parents had been kidnapped by the aliens.

"Mom and Dad should be home soon," said Luther, not very convincingly. "Meanwhile, let's make sure everything is locked." Even though it was warm outside and the house had no air conditioning, the kids closed and locked all the windows and bolted the front and back doors.

"Let's stay together here in the living room," said Chloe. "We can watch television." She turned on the TV set and saw nothing but a snowy picture on the screen. "The signal has been scrambled."

It's the UFO, thought Luther. *It's around here somewhere. But don't say anything. You'll scare the others.*

"Let's get something to read," Chloe suggested. "That will keep our minds busy."

The Ferguson children each grabbed a book or magazine and tried to read, but they couldn't focus on the words. All they could think about was the UFO and when it would come back again. No one thought in terms of *if* it would, only *when*.

It was nearly 10 P.M., and James and Matilda still had not arrived home. The kids knew their parents were two hours late, and each minute increased their worry.

Luther kept a vigil, looking out the window, waiting with hope for his parents—and with dread for the UFO—to return. He tried to keep his mind free from worry, but it was impossible. He began thinking about the day he was kidnapped by the UFO—the blinding light, the sheer terror, the examination, the strange aliens. He believed there was more, much more, that had happened to him, but his mind had blocked it out.

As he relived the abduction, his heart raced and his hands sweated. Looking up in the sky and waiting for something he didn't want to see was taking a toll on him. His head pounded and his body ached from stress. *I don't ever want to see those aliens again,* he told himself. *Please don't come back.* Every minute that passed only increased the tension. By 11 P.M., he couldn't stand it anymore and collapsed.

"Luther!" cried out Chloe. "Johnny, help me get him on the couch." They splashed water on him until he regained consciousness. "The stress got to me," Luther explained. "I'm sorry."

"You have nothing to be sorry about, Luther," said Chloe. "Just relax. We'll get through this—"

Bethany let out a scream. "I saw a flash of light!" Johnny looked through the window. "It's clouding up," he said. "It's probably lightning."

"Yeah, that was it," nodded Bethany, wishing he was right, but believing he was wrong.

As everyone returned to their seats, Chloe hushed them. "I heard something outside. Listen."

They all heard it. A faint thump . . . thump . . . thump coming from the front porch. "Footsteps," whispered Johnny.

"Are Mom and Dad home?" Bethany asked hopefully.

Johnny peered out the window. "No, they're not here yet. I don't see anyone outside."

Thump . . . thump . . . thump. Judging from the sound, the footsteps were now right outside the door.

"The aliens are back!" declared Luther. "Quick, get behind the couch." They huddled behind the furniture and waited for one minute, then another, and another. But they heard no more footsteps. Finally, Johnny stood up and carefully walked to the front door. He whipped it open, but no one was there. Cautiously, he and Luther stepped outside and looked both ways. Then they crept all the way around the house. They found nothing.

When they returned, Johnny locked and bolted the front door and announced, with a sigh of relief, "The coast is clear. It must have been an animal."

"Maybe a kangaroo," Bethany said.

The Ferguson kids gave a nervous laugh and settled back into their chairs, picked up their reading material, and—

The front door flew open by itself and banged against the wall, jarring the already-jittery family to its feet in a chorus of frightened shrieks. In a matter of seconds, the room turned bitter cold until the kids were shivering. Then, for some unexplained reason, they became overwhelmed with a feeling of terrible sadness. Luther, Johnny, Chloe, and Bethany broke down and wept. They cried for an entire minute. Not until the door slammed shut by itself and the room temperature returned to normal did they stop sobbing.

As they wiped away their tears and caught their breath, Luther exclaimed, "They're playing games with us. This is nothing but a sport to them."

"How do you know?" asked Chloe.

"I can't explain it. But just now I got a flashback of when I was in the UFO. I remember getting the feeling that they were evil."

"We've got to get out of here," said Johnny.

"Where can we go in the middle of the night?" Luther asked. "We'll be sitting ducks for sure."

"But if we stay here . . ."

"We have no choice."

"Oh, dear," exclaimed Chloe, "look at this room." Everyone had been so upset that no one had noticed the living room had been trashed. An invisible force had knocked pictures off the walls, shoved books and magazines off the tables, and toppled over a couple of chairs.

As they straightened up the room, the Ferguson kids experienced something even more bizarre. They relived the entire last five minutes—exactly as it had happened before!

The front door flew open by itself and banged against the wall. The room turned bitterly cold and the kids burst into tears. A minute later, the door slammed shut, the room warmed up instantly, and they stopped crying. They even said the exact same words they had before until they had finished straightening up the room. Then all four kids suffered a momentary blackout. When they recovered, they stared at each other in stunned bewilderment.

"Did I imagine this, or did we just repeat the last few minutes?" asked Chloe.

"It was like rewinding a video and then playing it again—only this was real life," said Johnny.

"See what I mean?" Luther said. "Those aliens are having fun at our expense. It's like we're characters in their own private video game."

"I think I'm going to go crazy!" cried Bethany, burying her head in her hands.

"That's exactly what they want to happen," said Luther. "We've got to remain strong mentally. And trust me, that's not easy at all."

Suddenly, the Ferguson kids felt another surge of

freezing air. Then a gray-hooded figure in a helmet with a mirrored mask flashed past them, zoomed around the room twice with its feet never touching the floor, and disappeared. The entire event took no more than five seconds—so fast that none of the kids had time to react until it was gone.

"What was that?" Johnny asked, rubbing his eyes in disbelief.

"It was an alien—just like the ones I saw in the UFO," replied Luther, slumping back in the chair.

"It came right through the wall!" Chloe said in wide-eyed amazement. "It didn't even use the door."

"I've never seen anyone move so fast," added Bethany.

"I want them to go away," sobbed Chloe. "To leave us alone. To let us live in peace."

Johnny put his hands to his head and asked, "Why is it doing this to us?"

Just then the hooded alien appeared in the corner of the room and began copying every move Johnny made. It put its hands on its head as Johnny had done. When he threw his hands up in the air in dismay, so did the alien. Johnny then stumbled backward and moved behind the couch. The alien pretended to do the same thing from across the room.

"Stop it!" demanded Luther, pointing to the alien. "Stop it and get out! Leave us alone!"

Luther, mustering up all the courage he could, took a couple of steps toward the alien, who then pulled out a small device that looked like an electric razor and pointed it at Luther. The boy immediately froze into a human statue.

"What have you done to my brother!" cried Chloe. She started to advance toward Luther when the alien pointed the device at Chloe and paralyzed her too.

By now the other two kids were scared beyond belief. Feeling totally helpless, they cowered in the corner, clutching each other and waiting to find out their own fate. The alien floated toward the ceiling, looked down at the two frightened kids and froze them too.

Although they couldn't move, the kids had full use of their minds. They knew what was happening. They could see each other and the alien. They simply couldn't budge or even blink. Then the alien went over to Luther and touched him in the forehead with the device. Luther could once again move. The alien did the same to the other three children before floating back to the corner with its arms folded.

A moment later, despite their unbelievable night of horror, the Ferguson kids behaved in the oddest way imaginable, given the circumstances. They burst out in uncontrollable laughter. They laughed so hard, they fell to the floor and rolled around. Tears streamed down their faces as they held their sides and tried to catch their breath. Every time they started to wind down from their laughter, one of them would look at the alien— who was still floating in the corner—and burst out laughing, which only caused the others to roar.

Their situation was hardly humorous—and they knew it. But they couldn't stop. They were totally helpless. The more they laughed, the more they hurt. Their sides seared with pain, their lungs and throats ached, and their eyes stung from the tears. It wasn't funny anymore. But still they laughed.

Their brains were in turmoil. In the deepest recesses of their minds, they knew they were in danger of dying laughing. They had to stop because they were finding it harder and harder to breathe. They were in fear for their lives. By now all the kids were curled up in balls on the floor, gasping for breath, until everything went black—and one by one they passed out.

* * *

"Luther, speak to me. Come on, son, wake up."

Luther opened his eyes and saw his father kneeling beside him, gently tapping him on the face. "Dad," he murmured. "Oh, I'm so glad to see you." Luther sat up and tried to clear his head. Quickly, he turned to see if everyone else was okay. Johnny, Chloe, and Bethany were also regaining consciousness.

"The alien —" Luther said anxiously.

"It's gone," replied James. "They're all gone."

"How do you know? How can you be sure?"

"On our way home, we were stopped by a UFO," James explained to his children. "We were scared to death. They paralyzed us and floated us up into their spaceship. The aliens examined us and took blood and skin samples. When they were finished, they pulled out a metal stick and placed the tip to our foreheads. It was amazing and horrifying at the same time. In our minds, we could see that an alien was harassing you kids at home. The cold temperatures, making you cry, zipping around the room, repeating the scene, and then forcing you to laugh until you passed out."

"It was so cruel," added Matilda. "Then we heard a message in our head from one of the aliens in the spaceship. It was something like, 'We have the power to make your reality whatever we want it to be. See what we can do with your children's minds?' And then our minds went blank."

"The next thing we remember," James continued, "we were driving down the road again."

"What makes you so sure they won't be terrorizing us any more?" Luther asked.

"Because at the end of the message we were told they were leaving now," answered James. "So everything will be all right."

James and Matilda hugged their weary, emotionally drained children. "Everything will be all right," echoed Matilda.

But neither parent had the heart to tell their kids that the message said one other thing: "We will return again someday."

THE ALIEN BOOK

About once a week over a six-month period, 12-year-old Katy Kelly experienced an eerie daydream. It would pop into her head at odd times—while she was riding in the school bus or watching TV or even taking a shower.

The daydream was always the same. Katy would wake up in the middle of the night to see two small unearthly people standing in her bedroom doorway. They had chalky gray skin, stood about three feet (.9 m) tall, had big heads, large almond-shaped eyes, and were dressed in tight gray outfits. One of the creatures pulled out a lighted wand and used it to draw neon purple squiggly lines and geometric figures in the air. The glowing writing remained suspended as if it had been drawn on a plate of glass. The lines and figures were nothing Katy had ever seen before. As she studied the figures, the little creatures and the writing in the air faded away.

Whenever she experienced one of these daydreams, Katy wondered why she would ever think of such a thing. She wasn't a big fan of science fiction. The popular space movies she had seen didn't do much for her. Katy couldn't come up with an explanation other than she must have read an article once in a magazine that had left a lasting impression in the back of her mind. She never mentioned these daydreams to anyone because she thought they sounded silly.

But then Katy saw something that made her suspect her frequent daydream was a clue to a mysterious and unsettling secret.

It happened after Katy had walked into the room of her 10-year-old sister Terry and asked to borrow a few sheets of writing paper. "I have plenty in my notebook on my desk," said Terry. "Help yourself."

Katy opened the notebook and took out a handful. As she was about to close it, she noticed the inside cover and was stunned by what she saw: two human-like creatures with big heads and almond-shaped eyes just like the ones in her daydream. Scattered around them were the familiar squiggly lines.

"Terry! Who are these funny-looking people?"

"Nothing, just some spacemen I draw to pass the time when class gets boring."

"Where did you get the idea to draw them?"

"I don't know. They sort of come into my head."

"And these weird lines?"

Terry shrugged her shoulders. "They're just doodles I draw without thinking. Why all the questions?"

"Terry, I've seen these spacemen and squiggly lines before. They're constantly in my mind."

"So? What's the big deal?"

"It could be a very big deal."

* * *

One evening, Katy was helping her father, Mitch, look through an old trunk in the basement for his high school yearbook, because he planned to attend a reunion the following week. The trunk was crammed with awards, albums, journals, and old love letters that Mitch and his wife Charlotte had kept since they first started dating.

Katy picked up a yellowed envelope, opened it, pulled out the letter and read out loud, "My dearest darling—"

Her father swiped the letter from her hands and smiled sheepishly. "You don't want to be reading all that mushy stuff between your mother and me. You might see that we were once pretty hot stuff. That would wreck your current image of us as old fuddy-duddys. Besides, these letters are private."

"Oh, Daddy, just one letter, okay?"

As she went to reach for another envelope, she caught a glimpse of a page that had slipped partially out of a journal. Written in pencil on the page was something oddly familiar. But before she could get a close look at it, the lights flickered and then went out, throwing the house into darkness. They found a flashlight by the workbench and went upstairs to the kitchen where they were met by Terry and Charlotte.

"Is it a power failure?" asked Charlotte.

"I checked the circuit breakers," replied Mitch.

"They're fine. It must be an outage throughout the area."

Katy went to the window and said, "Ooooh. Take a look." The family gazed outside and saw a curious pink light shining through the clump of trees that bordered their backyard. The light began switching back and forth from red to pink.

"What's going on, Daddy?" asked Terry.

"Oh, it's nothing," he replied. "Probably the power company's generator blew, and we're seeing the light from an electrical problem at the substation."

"I'm getting the creeps," said Terry.

"Okay, let's go into the dining room, and we'll light some candles and play cards," Charlotte suggested. "How about a game of hearts?"

Katy took one more look out the window and then froze in fear—and disbelief. Four human-like creatures, no bigger than grade schoolers, with big heads and long spindly arms and legs were walking toward the Kellys' back door! Even more incredible, they looked exactly like the ones Katy had seen in her daydreams!

"Mom, Dad," blurted Katy in a voice rising with fright, "little gray men . . ."

Suddenly, everything went black and silent for several seconds. When Katy regained her senses, she saw to her shock that the creatures were entering the house. What astonished her was how they did it. They didn't bother opening the back door. Instead, they walked right through the locked, solid oak door without damaging it—as though it wasn't even there!

The sight turned Katy's brain topsy-turvy. Nothing made any sense. She knew there were no such things as little gray men or people who can walk through closed doors.

The intruders silently marched inside, one following the other, and stopped in front of Katy. Her mind tried hard to grasp the scene. Standing before her were four gray-skinned creatures. They wore tight dark body suits with a design on their right shoulders that reminded her of a lying-down "S".

In the palm of his gloved hand, the leader held a softball-sized glass globe that gave off a bluish glow. As the creature turned his palm down, the ball began to move on its own and rolled along his fingers until it sat on the back of his hand. He waved the ball toward the dining room, and the lights came back on in the house.

Staring in awe at the intruders, Katy slowly backed away from the kitchen until she reached the dining room. Then she turned around and gasped in horror. Her parents and sister looked like human statues, frozen in a moment of time. Charlotte had a deck of cards in her hand, ready to shuffle. Terry sat with her elbows on the table and her chin resting on her hands. Mitch was in mid-stride, holding a lighted candle. None of her family members could move a muscle.

This seems so real, but it can't be happening, thought Katy. *What a nightmare! Wake up, Katy, wake up!* With trembling fingers, she pinched herself. "Ouch!" she yelped. *Uh, oh, this is no dream.* She felt so scared that she thought she was going to pass out.

The leader held up the glowing globe again and waved it in front of Katy's face. An instant later, her fear and disbelief were replaced by a calm acceptance of this bizarre visit.

The leader took a step forward and, without moving his mouth, said, "Katy, don't be afraid."

"I'm not anymore, but I don't know why I shouldn't be," she replied. "What have you done to my family?"

"They are fine. They are resting and are not in any danger."

"Am I?"

"No. We came to pay you a visit."

"Are you from another galaxy or something?"

"We are from a distance that cannot be easily explained to you," replied the alien.

Katy shook her head in amazement and said, "So, all this stuff about UFOs and aliens, it's real." After a long awkward pause, Katy didn't know what to say, so she said, "Oh, where are my manners? Can I fix you some food?"

The leader nodded. Katy led the visitors back into the kitchen, where she opened the cupboard and pulled out a loaf of bread and a jar of peanut butter. After she made a sandwich, she handed it to the leader. He studied it as the others gathered around him, and then he opened the sandwich, holding a slice of bread in each hand.

"This is not our kind of food," he told Katy. "Our food is knowledge. Do you have anything like that?"

"You mean like books or something?" She glanced around the room and noticed that her schoolbooks were still on the kitchen counter where she had left them earlier in the day. "Here's some brain food for you. But please don't eat them."

The leader took the textbooks—earth science, English, and math—and a teen magazine. He kept the science book and passed out the reading material to the others. Next, he held the book with one hand in front of his face and, with his other hand, flipped through the pages as fast as he could. His fellow aliens did the same thing with their reading material and then returned them to Katy.

"Did you read them already?" she asked.

"Yes," said the leader. "Is this what they teach you?"

"Yes, it is. All except the magazine. My teacher won't let us read that one in class."

"I have some food for thought for you," he told her. With his long arm, he reached behind his back and pulled out a thin green book from a pocket that stretched across his shoulder blades. He held out the book for Katy to take.

"Thank you," she said. It was the size of her science book although much thinner and lighter. The cover was made of a texture she had never felt before, a cross between soft metal and cotton. When Katy opened it up, the first page glowed like the overhead lights in a classroom.

"Wow, how does it do that?" she wondered out loud. Then she turned to the next page. It beamed with light too, but what she saw on the page caused her to exclaim, "I've seen these before!" It contained the same bright purple squiggly lines and weird geometric shapes that appeared in her daydreams!

Eagerly, she thumbed through the rest of the book. Each page shined brightly and featured the same kinds of markings. Yet they still made no sense to her. She moved her fingers lightly across the pages, which felt like smooth slick pieces of soft plastic rather than paper. But even though they glowed, there was no heat nor any apparent source for the light.

"What am I supposed to do with this book?" Katy asked the leader.

"Try to understand it."

"But how?"

"That is up to you," he replied.

"And if I can't understand it?"

"Then we must try another time."

"Can I show it to my family and friends?"

"This is for your eyes only. And for only a short while. You must take extremely good care of it."

"But I've never seen writing like this. I've never learned space language."

As Katy stood in the kitchen and stared at the book again, Terry began to twitch at the dining room table. She slowly stood up and, still in a trance, walked into the kitchen.

"Terry, you're moving!" said Katy with relief. "Are you all right?"

But Terry didn't respond. She kept walking straight toward the aliens. "What's the matter with her?" Katy asked the leader. "What have you done to her?"

"She will be fine," he replied. "She recovered sooner than I thought. I will make a slight adjustment." Holding the glowing ball, he waved it in front of Terry's face. She immediately turned around and returned to the dining room.

"Terry!" shouted Katy. "Talk to me. Say something." Katy waved her hands in front of her sister's face, but Terry paid no attention. Terry sat down at the table in the dining room where her parents were still locked in the same frozen positions.

"She and the others are at rest right now," the leader explained. "They probably will not remember anything about this evening. It's for their own good. It eliminates the stress and shock of our presence. We are now going to put you at rest."

"What about my family? What about me?"

"You will wake up tomorrow with no ill effects."

"What about the book?" she said, holding it up.

"Put it in a safe spot and study it. You do not have much time. But first you must get rest."

The leader waved the glowing ball in front of Katy and the rest of her family. Then, one by one, each member walked upstairs, got undressed, and went to sleep.

* * *

The next morning, Katy woke up and immediately felt sick to her stomach. She had recalled every detail of the night's extraordinary experience. Her whole body shook with a mix of emotions, from excitement to fear. She bolted out of bed and ran downstairs where her parents calmly were drinking coffee and reading the paper.

"Are you okay?" Katy asked breathlessly.

"Yes, of course," replied Charlotte. "Why wouldn't we be?"

"Because of what happened last night," Katy declared. Bewildered by her parents' calm reaction, she asked, "You do remember about last night, don't you?"

"You mean the blackout?"

"No, no," Katy said with growing annoyance and concern. "The little gray men. You had to have seen them. They were here, right here in this room!"

Charlotte's eyes widened, and she gave Mitch an alarmed look. He glanced back at her with a slight nod and then turned to Katy. "What are you talking about, Katy?" he asked. "Did you have a bad dream?"

"This was no dream, Daddy. I'm telling you that these gray men came right through the door, and they . . . they . . ." She stopped and told herself, *Mom and Dad don't remember because the aliens blocked it from their memories. If I go blabbing any more about this, they'll think I'm crazy.* She looked at her parents and shook her head. "You know, on second thought, it must have been a nightmare. There's no such thing as little gray men."

Katy wondered if Terry remembered anything, so she went back upstairs and woke her up. "Terry, did anything strange happen last night?"

"The house went dark," she replied.

"Anything else?"

"No, but I had a scary dream."

"About little gray men?"

"How did you know?"

"Did they come into the house and then make you and Mom and Dad stay still so you couldn't move?"

"Yes, and one of them held a shiny round light in his hand, and I started to walk toward him. But he made me go back to the dining room table."

"Terry, I'm going to tell you a secret, but you've got to promise not to tell anyone else." After Terry nodded, Katy continued, "That wasn't a dream you had. It was true. It really happened." She lowered her voice and in an excited whisper revealed, "They're spacemen!"

"Are they from Mars?"

"They're from far, far away."

"How do you know they're spacemen?"

"I have proof. Come with me."

With Terry following her, Katy returned to her bedroom and opened the top drawer of her dresser. Underneath a sweater, she pulled out the mysterious green book and handed it to Terry. The little girl opened it and jumped back when the first page glowed. "Oh, that's pretty. What is it?"

"It's a book given to me from the leader of the gray spacemen. But I don't know what it says."

Terry flipped through the pages and squealed, "It's got funny lines and designs in it—just like the ones I draw when I'm doodling. Why is that?"

Katy thought a moment and asked, "When did you start drawing them?"

"I think about six months ago."

"That's around the time I started daydreaming about them. Terry, I think these aliens have visited both of us before! We probably couldn't remember because they made us forget. That's what happened to Mom and Dad last night."

"I'm getting scared," said Terry.

"Me too. But I don't think the spacemen want to hurt us. I think they're trying to see how smart we are. That's why they gave me the book."

"What does it say?"

"I don't know. Let's see if we can figure it out together."

They looked at the front cover again. In the center was a gold geometric design that looked like several triangles jumbled together. Inside the book, which was about 20 pages thick, the lines and symbols appeared on only one side of each page. The first written page featured several curlicues, sideways parentheses, angled commas and dashes, curvy lines, dots, and strange symbols.

"How are we supposed to read this?" asked Terry.

"I don't know. It doesn't make any sense to me. I don't recognize any of the letters—if that's what they are—and the symbols aren't anything I've ever seen."

Pointing to one particular symbol, Terry said, "This looks like a smiley face on a box." She pointed to another and said, "And this looks like a broken arrow in a balloon."

"It's so hard," Katy moaned. "I'll never figure this out."

"Why don't you show Mom and Dad?"

"I can't do that. I'm not supposed to show this book to anyone—not even you."

"What are you going to do?"

"I don't know," said Katy, shaking her head in frustration. "I'll keep staring at it and try to make sense out of it. Now, remember, don't tell anyone about this."

After Terry left the room, Katy sat on the bed and thumbed back and forth through the pages. She hoped something would click in her mind to help her learn the secrets of the alien book. After nearly an hour, she began to feel a soft vibration in her head. New and different thoughts began popping into her brain every so often. *Open your mind . . . the planet must be saved . . . know yourself . . . the human race has the power to change . . . other worlds must help . . .*

Two hours of intense concentration left Katy with an aching head and stinging eyes. *I've had it with this book,* she told herself. *No more. I just don't get it.* She put the book back in the drawer under her sweater and went for a walk.

About 9 P.M. that evening, Katy joined the rest of the family sitting at the kitchen table, looking over Mitch's old high school yearbook. As soon as she sat down, the lights in the house dimmed and then went out. A pink light shined through the window.

"Oh, no, they've come back!" shouted Katy. No one else said a word and Katy quickly discovered why. Her parents and Terry were once again paralyzed right where they sat. Katy wheeled around and saw the same four aliens from the previous night standing in the kitchen. The leader was holding the glowing ball.

"What do you want from me?" she asked fearfully.

"Tell me what you learned from the book."

"I've tried to figure out what it says, but it's impossible. I mean, I can't read alien writing. I guess it's about stuff like the human race and saving the planet, but it's mostly mumbo jumbo to me. It's too hard."

"Then it is not your time," said the leader. "However, there will be other opportunities."

"Can't I just ask you questions, and you give me the answers instead?"

"The book explains all you need to know."

"Well, at least tell me why you're here."

"To help humans and the galaxies. We visit people like you all over this planet and feed them, if they are ready, with the knowledge that will help save this planet."

"Why have you come to my house? Why not an important person or a real brain?"

"All people are important and all have a brain."

"How many have you visited? Hundreds? Thousands?"

"Many more."

"Then why haven't they told the rest of us or gone on TV?"

"Most can't recall the visits, because we've put a block on their memory. The block doesn't always work—like your case—or it leaves the memory of the visit somewhat fuzzy, like in your sister's case. Those people who do remember will speak up when the time is right."

"About six months ago, I started having daydreams about aliens, and Terry began doing space drawings. Is that when you first visited us?"

"Yes."

"I guess we had trouble remembering it, although it was always in the back of our mind."

"It is time for us to go. We will be back soon."

"How soon is soon?"

The alien did not answer. Instead, he waved the glowing ball, and the Kelly family went upstairs to bed.

* * *

Katy woke up the next morning remembering her second encounter with the aliens. She simply couldn't keep this incredible event quiet. At breakfast, she announced to her parents, "We had another visit last night."

"What are you talking about, dear?" asked Charlotte.

"Aliens from another planet. You were here, Mom.

You had to have seen them before they froze you."

"But how could that be?" asked her perplexed father.

"What do you think happened last night?" asked Katy.

"We were looking at my old yearbook when we had another brief power outage."

"What happened next?" she asked.

"Well, I, I don't remember. I must have fallen asleep," said her father.

"What about you, Mom?" asked Katy.

"I guess I fell asleep too. Katy, why do you believe we were visited by aliens?"

"Because I have proof," Katy replied confidently. "I'll show you something that didn't come from this world."

Katy dashed upstairs, opened her drawer, and rummaged around her sweaters, looking for the alien book. But it wasn't there. Frantically, Katy tried the next drawer and the next one. *Where is it? Where could it be? I don't believe this! It was here last night.*

She rushed into Terry's room. "Terry, did you take the alien book?"

"No, I didn't. Why?"

"It's gone!"

"The aliens were here last night, weren't they?" asked Terry. "At first, I thought it was a dream, but it wasn't. I kind of remember seeing four of them in the kitchen talking to you. I bet you they took it."

"You're probably right. I told Mom and Dad about the visit, but they don't believe me. I've got to find that book. It's the only proof I have. All those markings and symbols and—" Katy stopped in mid-sentence and yelled, "The trunk! I just remembered. I might have seen some alien writing in a journal in Dad's trunk in the basement the other day!"

Katy raced to the basement, threw open the trunk, and searched for the journal. Under a dusty pile of letters and books, she found an old notebook. She pulled it out, opened it up—and gasped. Written in pencil on two loose pages were the same squiggly lines and geometric designs that appeared in the alien book!

Clutching the two pages with both hands, Katy dashed upstairs to the kitchen and confronted her parents. "What's this?" she demanded.

Surprised by Katy's discovery, Mitch said, "You shouldn't be looking at this."

"Daddy, I'm sorry. I know it was wrong of me to go through your trunk, but this strange writing is the same kind I saw in the book the aliens gave me."

"You actually saw the green book?" asked Charlotte.

"Yes, it was given to me two nights ago, when we were visited by those little gray men. But now it's gone." Katy thought a moment and asked, "Wait, how did you know the book was green?"

Her mother sighed and looked at Mitch. He nodded. "Sit down, Katy," said Charlotte. "I guess it's time you knew the truth. Your father and I have something incredible to tell you."

Charlotte paused to collect her thoughts. "Years ago, before you were born, we were visited by the 'grays.' That's what we called the aliens."

Mitch then picked up the story. "They gave us the green book to study, but we didn't understand any of it. A day later, they came back and took the book away. I wrote down what I could remember from the first couple of pages of the book. I thought about showing the copies to an authority, but I was afraid they'd think I was a kook. Besides, Mom was dead set against me showing it to anyone."

"Even though the aliens never harmed us, I was terrified of them," added Charlotte. "I urged Dad not to do anything with his copies. I just wanted the aliens to leave us alone, so he stuffed the copies in the trunk, and we tried to forget about them. I prayed the aliens would never return. But now they've come back to visit you, even though we have no memory of it. And they've shown you the green book."

"But I didn't understand it."

"Join the club, honey," said her father.

"What do you think the book is about?" Katy asked.

"We may never know," Mitch replied. "But I believe it's a blueprint prepared by the aliens for us humans to save our planet. The book probably gives off some sort of energy that sends a message that only a few special people can pick up in their minds."

"I really want to be one of those people, Daddy."

"Someday, Katy, maybe you will."